CHUNKY KNITS

CHUNKY KNITS

14 quick and easy step-by-step projects

Carolyn Clewer

NORTH LIGHT BOOKS
Cincinnati, Ohio

A QUARTO BOOK

Distributed to the trade and
art markets in North America by
North Light Books,
an imprint of F&W Publications, Inc.
4700 East Galbraith Road
Cincinnati, OH 45236
(800) 289-0963

ISBN 1-58180-446-6

Conceived, designed, and produced by
Quarto Publishing plc
The Old Brewery
6 Blundell Street
London N7 9BH

PROJECT EDITOR: Nadia Naqib
ART EDITOR: Anna Knight
ASSISTANT ART DIRECTOR: Penny Cobb
DESIGNER: Penny Dawes
TEXT EDITORS: Sue Richardson and
Pauline Hornsby
PHOTOGRAPHERS: Paul Forrester and
Colin Bowling
ILLUSTRATOR: Kuo Kang Chen

ART DIRECTOR: Moira Clinch
PUBLISHER: Piers Spence

QUAR.CKNI

Manufactured by Universal Graphics
Pte Ltd, Singapore
Printed by Leefung-Asco Printers Ltd, China

Contents

Introduction   6

Getting Started

Materials and Equipment   10

Basic Skills   14

Projects

Project 1: Woolly Winter Scarf   34

Project 2: Hippie Shoulder Bag   38

Project 3: Man's Raglan Rollover   42

Project 4: Ladies' Turtleneck Raglan   48

Project 5: Chunky Cardigan   52

Stitch Techniques   58

Poodle Loop Stitch   60

Cabling   62

Project 6: Blackberry Bomber   64

Project 7: Afghan Coat   72

Project 8: Kids' Poncho   78

Project 9: Lacy Cowl Neck Sweater   82

Project 10: Cable V-neck   88

Fair Isle   94

Intarsia   96

Project 11: Snowflake Style   98

Project 12: Man's Intarsia Sweater   106

Embellishing Techniques   112

Embroidery   114

Project 13: Beaded Sweater   116

Project 14: Sequinned Shawl   122

Reading Patterns   126

Index & Credits   128

CHUNKY KNITS

Introduction

Knitwear has always played an influential role in fashion trends and its latest manifestation is in the form of chunky knits. Whether you are an ardent follower of fashion or a knitting enthusiast, you cannot have failed to notice the impact that chunky knits have had on the catwalk in recent seasons.

The current revival of interest in both handicrafts and individuality has inspired fashion designers to update and scale up the traditional techniques of hand knitting. This book shows you just how easy it is to re-create this visual and textural impact, while retaining the practical qualities of warmth and comfort offered by knitwear.

Using very little knitting know-how and armed with chunky yarn and needles, the complete novice will soon be guided through simple, practical, and creative projects that are surprisingly fast to knit.

This book guides you from the beginning, introducing new techniques project by project with step-by-step pictures. The book is designed to be worked through in order; different skills are introduced as they are needed. The beginner will learn the basics, from casting on and knitting the first stitch to shaping and finishing work professionally. Each topic is clearly explained and presented with step-by-step photography, showing the simplest ways of achieving successful results.

Once you have explored the techniques in the starter projects, you will be introduced to a range of simple textural stitch patterns, ranging from open lacy knits and loopy trims to giant-sized cable detailing. Learn how to interpret the growing trend for eclectic and colorful pattern, as you discover Fair Isle and intarsia techniques.

Chunky knits can be embellished and customized with colorful beading, sequins, or embroidery. These simple techniques will help you to personalize and decorate your work.

With the help of this book you should gain the skills and confidence to try working from other knitting patterns. You may wish to make all of the projects, or you may prefer to practice the different techniques on smaller test swatches as you work your way through the book.

Knitting has been around since 1000 BC, but it's never been more fashionable than now. How else can you simultaneously transform your wardrobe and escape the stresses of 21st-century life? The exciting and growing range of chunky and super chunky yarns that are currently available will provide inspiration for inventing and adapting ideas with texture and color combinations of your own. So the time is right to invest in chunky needles and yarn, a few basic skills, some leisure time—and get knitting!

Carolyn Clewer

GETTING STARTED

GETTING STARTED

Materials and Equipment

If you have a ball of yarn and a pair of knitting needles then you will be able to knit. However, to achieve successful results, it is important to choose the right materials and equipment for any project. The projects in this book concentrate on using chunky and super chunky needles and yarn, which are quick and fun to work with. You probably already have some of the other equipment needed like a tape measure and scissors, but as you work through the projects, you will probably find it useful to buy more specialist accessories.

Yarn fiber

Any continuous thread can be used to knit, but most knitting yarns are made by spinning strands of fiber together. Fibers may be natural or manmade, and many yarns are made from a combination of different fibers. The fiber content of yarn will have a big impact on the way that the finished fabric behaves, how well it wears, and how it should be cared for.

Natural fibers include those made from animal origins, like wool, mohair, silk, alpaca, and angora. Wool produced from sheep is traditionally the most popular yarn for hand knitting as it is easily worked with and produces an elastic, durable, and warm fabric. Wool is not usually machine washable unless it has been specially treated or combined with a synthetic fiber.

Natural fibers made from plants include cotton and linen, which are cool to wear and easy to wash. Cotton is less elastic than wool and tends to show any irregularities of stitch.

Synthetic fibers are often used to emulate natural fibers at a cheaper cost but are progressively being used to produce new effects and fancy yarns. They are often machine washable but do not generally respond well to heat and may easily lose spring and elasticity. They should therefore be blocked or pressed carefully.

Yarn weights and types

Most yarns are made by twisting several threads together in a process known as spinning. Combining different fibers, colors, and spinning techniques in a variety of ways can create endless texture combinations. Yarns can also be produced by knitting fine threads together, making tape and chainette yarns, or by trapping short threads into the core yarn, making chenille and tufted yarns. Any continuous length of thread can be used for knitting. You can experiment with raffia, ribbon, and even string.

Yarn weights or thicknesses will affect the choice of needles to be used and the consequent gauge of the knitting. Over the years, certain yarn descriptions and categories have evolved to make it easier to identify standard weights of yarn. The yarns available in each category are not necessarily similar to look at, but they can be knitted to a similar gauge. As fashions change, new yarn types become more popular. Many years ago a fisherman (Aran) weight yarn was considered to be a thick yarn but, with the recent development and popularity of chunky and, now, super chunky yarns, fisherman is considered to be a medium weight yarn.

The descriptions of weight for heavier yarns are less established and so the ball band information will be a more useful guide than the yarn description given by the spinner. Two or more ends of finer yarn can be knitted together to make a heavier weight. Needle sizes are given as a guide—the thicker the yarn, the bigger the needles. Some novelty yarns give a guide to equivalent weight, for example, "knits as chunky."

Super chunky wool

Super chunky wool mix

Super chunky slubby wool

Extra chunky wool mix

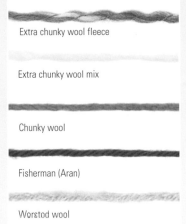

Extra chunky wool fleece

Extra chunky wool mix

Chunky wool

Fisherman (Aran)

Worsted wool

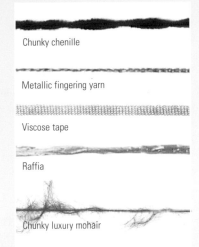

Chunky chenille

Metallic fingering yarn

Viscose tape

Raffia

Chunky luxury mohair

Yarns are available in a wide range of fibers, thicknesses, and textures, from chunky mohair to fine metallics.

Super chunky yarn is a really fat yarn best knitted on giant needles. Use size 15–36 (10–20 mm) needles.

Extra chunky yarn is thicker than a standard chunky and is faster to knit. Use size 11–15 (8–10 mm) needles.

Chunky yarn is a thick yarn often used for warm winter sweaters. Use size 10–11 (6–8 mm) needles.

Fisherman (Aran) is a medium weight yarn traditionally used for cable designs. Use size 8 or 9 (5 or 5 ½ mm) needles.

Worsted wool is slightly thinner than Fisherman and should be knitted on size 6 or 7 (4 or 4 ½ mm) needles.

4-ply yarn is a finer weight than double knit and is knitted on thin needles, size 3 (3 or 3 ½ mm).

Fingering yarn is very fine and designed for crochet work.

Fancy yarns like metallic, shiny, chenille, and tape yarns come in all sorts of thicknesses and can give exciting effects to your knitting, used alone or combined with other yarns.

Fluffy yarns like mohair are usually designed to be knitted more loosely. Kid mohair is finer and can be knitted like 4-ply or DK. Luxury or chunky mohair should be knitted to the same gauge as chunky yarn although the strand is finer.

Ball band information

Most yarn comes in balls or hanks, which are labeled with lots of information on a ball band. If you read the ball band carefully, you will find out everything you need to know about the yarn.

Manufacturer's name and yarn type This tells you what the yarn is called and which spinner made it.

Weight and length This will help you work out how many balls of yarn you need to knit your project or pattern.

Fiber content This tells you what the yarn is made of.

Shade This is the manufacturers name for or number of the yarn color.

Dye lot This is a number indicating which balls of yarn were dyed at the same time. If you are using more than one ball of yarn in the same shade, make sure that they have the same shade number so that they are an exact match.

Needle size This is the recommended needle size for the yarn. It is a good guide, but if your knitting is tight you may need to use a bigger needle size. If your knitting is loose,

you may need to use a smaller needle size in order to achieve the correct gauge.

Gauge The gauge helps you work out the number of stitches and rows you need to get your knitting the right size. Stitches knitted in thin yarn or with thin needles are smaller than stitches knitted in thick yarn or with thick needles (see page 28).

Washing instructions This information is usually shown as symbols which explain how you should wash and care for your knitting.

Other materials You will often need to use other trims and fastenings to finish a garment. The choice of trim can play a big part in the look of the finished garment. Make sure that the washing or care instructions of trims are compatible with the yarn used, and that the size and weight is appropriate to the knitted fabric.

CHUNKY KNITS

Equipment

You will need some basic equipment before you start knitting, but other items can be collected gradually as you need them. A pair of knitting needles is the most essential piece of equipment. Chunky weight needles are usually made from plastic, but needles can also be made from metal, bamboo, or wood. Thrift stores are a great place to pick up needles of different types and sizes as you are building up your collection. Always use a needle gauge to check the size of second-hand needles, as the sizing system has changed over the years and varies between different countries. The length of needles can vary to suit the number of stitches being worked and the method of holding needles that you prefer (see page 15). Avoid needles that are bent or rough or have blunt or broken ends, as they will hamper your technique and may damage the yarn.

▼ **Knitting needles** come in matching pairs in a range of sizes to suit different yarn weights, from size 0 (2 mm), which are very fine, to size 36 (20 mm), which are very thick.

▲ **A needle gauge** is used to check the size of knitting needles.

▶ **Cable needles** are small double-pointed needles that are used to hold stitches when working cables.

▲ **Double-pointed needles or circular needles** are also available and are used for knitting in the round.

▼ **Stitch holders** are used to temporarily hold stitches to be knitted at a later stage.

▶ **Stitch markers** are small plastic or metal rings that can be slipped into the knitting or onto a needle to mark a particular stitch or row.

▶ **A row counter** can be fitted close to the knob of a straight needle to keep count of the number of rows you have worked in the pattern. Simply turn the dial every time you finish a row.

▶ **Safety pins** can be used for holding a small number of stitches and are also useful for pinning seams to be sewn.

▲ **Large-headed dressmaker's pins** are essential when blocking pieces to size and for pinning seams. Choose the longest pins that you can find when working with chunky yarns.

◀ **Crochet hooks** are useful for picking up dropped stitches and for making trims.

▶ **A blunt-ended needle** with an eye large enough to fit the yarn is needed for sewing up knitting. Finer needles may be needed for sewing zippers and trims.

▼ **Sharp scissors** are essential for cutting yarn.

Needle size conversion chart

US	Metric (mm)	Old UK/ Canadian
36	20	–
19	15	–
17	12	–
15	10	000
13	9	00
11	8	0
10½	7½	1
10½	7	2
10½	6½	3
10	6	4
9	5½	5
8	5	6
7	4½	7
6	4	8

▶ **Needle point protectors** can be used to prevent stitches falling off the needles when not in use.

◀ **A tape measure** is an essential piece of equipment. Replace regularly as old tape measures can stretch and become inaccurate.

▶ **A mohair brush** is used to raise the pile of mohair fabric.

▶ **Bobbins** are used to hold small amounts of yarn for intarsia knitting.

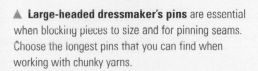

CHUNKY KNITS

Getting Ready to Knit

When learning to knit, it is important to work in a comfortable, calm, and well-lit environment, working with yarn and needles that are easy to use. Choose a chunky weight yarn that is smooth and plain colored, so that each stitch will be clearly defined. Very decorative or fluffy yarns can be distracting when learning the basics. Find the end of the yarn in the center of the ball and pull this end out to work with, so that the ball does not roll about as you knit. Look at the ball band for a guide to recommended needle sizes and choose a pair of needles that is suitable for your yarn. Needle length is a matter of choice, but generally shorter length needles such as 10 or 12 in. (25 or 30 cm) are easier for a beginner to handle.

Making a slip knot

Making a slip knot is always the first stage of casting on. The slip knot is then placed on the left-hand needle to form the first cast-on stitch.

1 Grip the loose end of yarn in your hand with your palm facing toward you and wrap the working end (coming from the ball) of yarn around your first two fingers.

2 Wrap the yarn around the fingers again, crossing the first loop so the second loop is nearer your hand.

3 Hold both ends of yarn against your palm and with the finger and thumb of your other hand, reach down into the first loop and pull the second loop through.

4 Hold this loop with one hand and pull the loose end of yarn gently with the other hand to tighten the knot, before slipping onto the needle.

Holding Yarn and Needles

There are many different ways of holding needles and yarn—the most important thing is to find a way that is comfortable for you. The most common techniques are to hold the yarn in the right hand and the right-hand needle with either the pen-hold/free-needle method or the knife-hold/fixed-needle method. Experiment with different methods to see which you prefer. Don't be put off, as holding the needles will undoubtedly feel a little awkward at first, but with practice you will be able to work much more quickly and instinctively with any of the methods described.

Holding the yarn

In order to feed the yarn evenly, it must be tensioned as it runs through your fingers. The forefinger is used to move the yarn around the tip of the needle when making a stitch.

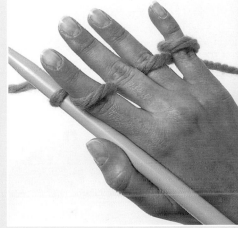

Left hand

▶ To hold the yarn in your left hand, take the working yarn over the little finger, under the next two fingers and around the forefinger.

Right hand

▶ A simple way for a beginner to hold the yarn in the right hand is to wrap the working yarn (coming from the ball) around the little finger, over the next finger, under the middle finger, and over the forefinger.

Holding the needles

Pen hold

The needles used for this method can be as short as are practical. Tension the yarn through your fingers and hold the right-hand needle like a pen, balanced on top of the hand, between the thumb and forefinger. Hold the left-hand needle with the hand over the top and use the thumb and forefinger of the left hand to hold the tip of the right needle.

Knife hold

This method can be used with short or long needles. If using long needles, some knitters like to hold the right-hand needle under the arm against the body, leaving the right hand free when making a stitch. Tension the yarn through your fingers and hold the right hand over the needle like a knife. Hold the left hand needle lightly in the same way.

CHUNKY KNITS

Casting On

Casting on is the first step of knitting. It is the process of making your first row of stitches on a needle. There are several different ways of casting on, but making a slip knot is always the first stage. Alternative ways of casting on can be used for different types of knitting. Different techniques can give a firm, stretchy, or loose edge to your knitting.

One-needle cast-on (thumb method)

This method is very easy and produces a stretchy edge. It is suitable for less elastic yarns like cottons and also when casting on separate collars and trims that will be sewn into place.

1 Slide the slip knot onto a knitting needle and gently tighten it, to form your first stitch. Hold your needle in one hand and grip the working end of yarn with the fingers of the other hand.

2 Wrap the working end of yarn around your thumb so that it forms a loop.

3 Push the tip of the needle up through the loop on your thumb.

4 Slip your thumb out of the loop and gently pull the working yarn to tighten the new stitch on the needle. When tightening the stitches make sure that they are still loose enough to slide up and down the needle easily.

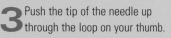

5 Repeat this process until you have the right number of stitches on your needle.

Two-needle cast-on (cable method)

This cast-on method produces a neat, firm edge. It is very versatile and is suitable for most fabrics, particularly rib and stockinette stitch edges.

1 Slide the slip knot onto the needle in your left hand, holding the short tail of yarn out of the way, under your fingers. Holding the ball end of yarn tensioned through your fingers, insert the tip of the right-hand needle up into the stitch from left to right.

2 Pass the yarn counterclockwise around the back of the right needle then back between the points of the two needles.

3 Use the tip of the right needle to draw the new loop of yarn through the slip knot on the left needle, toward you.

4 You have now formed a new stitch on the right needle.

5 Insert the tip of the left needle up into the new stitch and withdraw the right needle so that you have two stitches on the left needle.

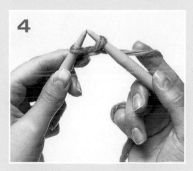

6 Insert the tip of the right needle behind the left needle, between the previous two stitches and gently tighten the yarn. Wind the yarn counterclockwise around the right needle, pull the new loop through, and transfer it to the left needle as before.

7 Repeat step 6 until you have the required number of stitches on the left needle.

Professional tips

When casting on, try not to work too tightly. There should be enough room to insert the tip of a needle into each cast-on stitch, or you will find it difficult to knit the first row. While learning, it is easier to work a little more loosely.

To make a looser, less solid edge, insert the right needle into the loop of the last stitch made, rather than behind it. This method is suitable for lace knitting or if the cast-on edge is to be sewn as a seam.

CHUNKY KNITS

Starting to Knit

Knit and purl stitches form the basis of all knitted fabrics. Each stitch is made by using the right needle to draw a loop of yarn through a stitch on the left-hand needle. Begin by casting on 15–20 stitches onto your left needle, ready to practice the knit stitch (see pages 16–17).

The knit stitch (abbreviated as k)

The knit stitch is the most basic and simple stitch to learn. Once you have practiced the two-needle cast-on (see page 17), you will notice that the knit stitch is made with a very similar action. Each stitch is formed by drawing a loop of yarn toward you, through the original stitch.

1 Hold the yarn and needles in the way you find most comfortable, with the cast-on stitches pushed up toward the tip of the left needle and the yarn tensioned through your fingers (see page 15). Hold the yarn behind the right needle. Insert the tip of the right needle from front to back, up into the first stitch on the left needle, so that the tip of the right needle crosses behind the left.

2 Use your forefinger to carry the yarn counterclockwise, around the back of the right needle and between the two needles from left to right.

3 With the tip of the right needle, draw the loop of yarn through the first stitch on the left needle, toward you. This creates a new loop on the right needle.

4 Slip the original stitch off the left needle so that you have completed the knit stitch.

5 Repeat this process into each of the stitches on the left needle until you have completed a row of knit stitches. Turn the work around so that you are holding the needle with the stitches on it in your left hand. Knit another row in the same way. Continue to knit each row of stitches in this manner, and you will see that the resulting elastic fabric, known as garter stitch, has the same appearance on both sides.

The purl stitch (abbreviated as p)

The purl stitch is the other stitch that forms the basis of all knitting. Each stitch is made by drawing a loop of yarn away from you, through the original stitch. Purl can seem slightly more difficult than knit stitch at first, but the result is just like a knit stitch made facing the opposite direction. Once you have mastered both knit and purl, you can progress to stockinette, rib, and other stitch patterns. Begin by casting on 15–20 stitches onto your left needle ready to practice the purl stitch.

1 Hold the yarn and needles in the way you find most comfortable, with the cast-on stitches pushed up toward the tip of the left needle and the yarn tensioned through your fingers (see page 15). Hold the yarn in front of the right needle. Insert the tip of the right needle from back to front, down into the first stitch on the left needle, so that the tip of the right needle crosses in front of the left.

2 Use your forefinger to wrap the yarn counterclockwise around the back of the right needle tip and round to the front again.

3 Use the tip of the right needle to draw the loop of yarn back through the stitch on the left needle. This creates a new loop on the right needle.

4 Slip the original stitch off the left needle to complete the first purl stitch.

5 Repeat this process into each stitch on the left needle until a row has been worked. Turn the work and purl another row. You will notice that purling every row of the work looks the same as garter stitch (knitting every row). When you start to combine knit and purl stitches, more stitch patterns can be created.

CHUNKY KNITS

Stitch Patterns

Combining knit and purl stitches can form different stitch patterns. The most commonly used are stockinette, which knits up quickly and smoothly, and rib, which is often used for creating elastic edges to knitted garments, because it pulls the fabric in and does not roll up at the edges.

Stockinette stitch

Stockinette stitch is the most well-known combination of knit and purl. It is formed by alternating one row of knit stitches with one row of purl stitches, creating a smooth fabric. The right side of stockinette is characterized by rows of v-shaped stitches. The knit row is the right-side row of stockinette, as the smooth v-patterned side of the work is facing you as this row is being worked. The other side of stockinette is ridged and faces you on a wrong-side row (when completing a purl row). Instructions for stockinette usually begin by working the knit row.

Reverse stockinette stitch

The wrong side of stockinette is the purl side—the bumpy or ridged side facing you as you work a purl row. This is known as reverse stockinette when used as the right side. Instructions for reverse stockinette usually begin by working a purl row.

Rib structures

Rib structures are created by knitting and purling stitches within the same row, creating alternate vertical lines of smooth knit stitches and bumpy purl stitches on the front of the work. This makes a springy fabric that stretches across the width and does not curl up at the edges; it is therefore often used as a border such as a bottom edge, cuff, or neckband. Ribs are often worked on smaller needles than stockinette stitch fabric to create a tighter, neater finish. To create a ribbed fabric, the stitches that are knitted on row 1 are purled on row 2 and vice versa.

Single rib (k1, p1)
Cast on an even number of stitches.
Row 1 *K1, p1, repeat from * to end.
Repeat this row.

Double rib (k2, p2)
Cast on a multiple of four stitches.
Row 1 *K2, p2, repeat from * to end.
Repeat this row.

More stitch patterns

Other stitch patterns can be made by combining knit and purl in different ways. Seed stitch is often used for firm, non-elastic edges and trims, as it lays flat and has a bumpy texture. The stitches that are knitted on the first (right-side) row are also knitted on the second (wrong-side) row, and the stitches that are purled on the first row are also purled on the second row. This creates reverse stitches, alternating both horizontally and vertically. Note that the pattern is the same as for single rib, but with an extra stitch to create an odd number of stitches, giving a completely different effect. This structure looks the same on the right and wrong sides.

Seed stitch

Cast on an odd number of stitches.
Row 1 *K1, p1, repeat from * to last stitch, k1.
Repeat this row.

Joining New Yarn

You will need to join yarn to change color or when a ball is about to run out. Always join yarn at the beginning of a row. To be sure that you have enough yarn to complete a row, make sure that the yarn remaining measures four times the width of the work for most stitch patterns. If you are using a very textured stitch pattern, you may need more yarn. In this case, at the beginning of a row, when you think that you have enough yarn left for two more rows, tie a slip knot exactly half way along the remaining yarn and work the row. If you reach the slip knot before you complete the row, undo it and continue to the end of the row and join new yarn for the next row.

To help keep good stitch tension when starting a new ball of yarn, the new yarn can be tied around the original yarn. The knot can be undone when you are weaving in the ends of yarn, after the piece is finished (see page 29).

Tie the new yarn around the end of the original yarn, leaving a tail of about 6 in. (15 cm). Slide the knot right up to the next stitch to be worked and begin the next row with the new ball of yarn. Hold the tail of yarn in your hand, out of your way, for the first few stitches.

CHUNKY KNITS

Binding Off

This is the easiest way of securing the stitches once you have completed your last row of knitting. Binding off is also used to finish a group of stitches to shape the work. Binding off should stretch about as much as the rest of the knitting. It is important that it is not too tight, particularly for an edge that needs to be stretched, such as a neckband. Binding off should be worked "knitwise" on a knit row or "purlwise" on a purl row. If binding off other structures, keep in pattern, such as binding off "ribwise" after a rib row.

Binding off knitwise

1 Knit the first two stitches to be bound off in the normal way. Insert the tip of the left needle into the bottom stitch on the right needle.

2 Lift the stitch over the top stitch and off the end of the right needle.

3 One stitch remains on the right needle and the first stitch has been bound off.

4 Knit the next stitch so that there are two stitches on the right needle. Lift the bottom stitch over the top stitch as step 2, leaving one stitch on the right needle. Repeat this process until the required number of stitches has been bound off. If not binding off all the stitches, for example, for armhole shaping, continue knitting across the row. If binding off all the stitches, one stitch will remain on the right needle. Cut the yarn leaving a tail of about 6 in. (15 cm).

5 Remove the needle and thread the tail of yarn through the last stitch. Pull the tail tightly to secure.

Binding off purlwise

Instructions may require you to bind off stitches purlwise; simply purl the first two stitches as usual and follow the instructions for binding off knitwise, purling stitches instead of knitting them.

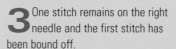

Shaping

Knitting can be shaped as the fabric is created. Increasing or decreasing the number of stitches in a row will make the fabric wider or narrower as desired. Shaping usually takes place at the beginning or end of a row but can also be worked into the middle of the knitting. There are several different methods explained here, each useful for shaping different parts of a garment or giving different detail to the work. Increases and decreases can be worked one or more stitches in from the beginning or end of a row, giving a neater edge for picking up stitches and sewing up. This technique, known as "fully fashioned," can be used as decorative detailing.

Increasing

Increasing the amount of stitches in a row will make the knitting wider. The general abbreviation for increasing is inc.

Bar increase knitwise (knit into front and back of stitch, abbreviated as kfb)

1 Insert the tip of the right needle into the stitch as if to knit.

2 Knit this stitch in the usual way, but do not let it slip off the left needle.

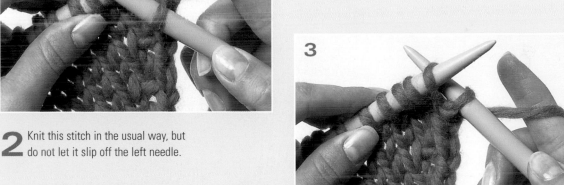

3 Insert the tip of the right needle into the back of the same stitch on the left needle, from right to left.

4 Wrap the yarn counterclockwise around the tip of the right needle and pull the new stitch through, creating another stitch on the right needle. Slip the original stitch off the left needle. You have created two stitches out of the original stitch. The increase is visible as a bar beneath the second stitch.

CHUNKY KNITS

Bar increase purlwise (purl into front and back of stitch, abbreviated as pfb)

1 Insert the tip of the right needle into the stitch as if to purl.

2 Purl this stitch in the usual way, but do not let it slip off the left needle.

3 Insert the tip of right needle into the back of the same stitch, from right to left (making sure that the right needle ends up in front of the left).

4 Wrap the yarn counterclockwise around the needle again and purl the stitch. Slip the original stitch off the left needle. You have created two stitches out of the original stitch. The increase is visible as a bar beneath the second stitch.

Lifted strand increase

This method is often used when increasing in the middle of a row as it is a very neat increase. The strand between two stitches is lifted from the previous row, and a stitch is worked into the back of it, never the front, in order to avoid a hole being formed.

Making a stitch by working into back of loop knitwise (abbreviated as m1 tbl)

1 Work to the place where the increase is required and insert the tip of the right-hand needle under the horizontal strand or loop between the stitches, from front to back.

2 Insert the tip of the left needle from front to back through the loop and transfer the loop to the left-hand needle.

3 Insert the tip of the right needle into the back of this new stitch, from right to left. The loop should now be twisted on the left needle as shown.

4 Knit into the loop in the usual way, thereby making an extra stitch on the right needle, and slip the loop off the left needle.

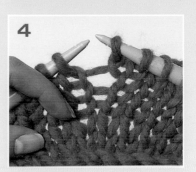

Purlwise

On a purl row, follow the first two steps of the technique for making a stitch on a knit row, then continue as follows:

1 Insert the right needle from back to front (left to right) into the back of the loop.

2 Purl into the back of the loop, thereby creating an extra stitch on the right needle, and slip the loop off the left needle.

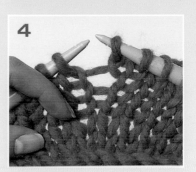

Increasing multiple stitches

A simple cast-on increase can be used to increase multiple stitches at the edge of the knitting. This uses the same technique as a thumb cast-on (see page 16).

Hold the needle with the stitches on it in your right hand and wrap the working yarn counterclockwise around your left thumb. Insert the tip of the right needle up into the loop from right to left and slip the loop onto the right needle. Pull gently to tighten and repeat for each new stitch required.

CHUNKY KNITS

Decreasing

Decreasing the number of stitches in a row will make the knitting narrower in order to form garment shaping, or as part of a decorative stitch structure. The decreased stitches form a slope that leans to right or left, depending on the technique used. If decreased stitches are used in a decorative way, it is usual to match the slopes produced on left and right for symmetry. The simplest way of decreasing stitches is by knitting or purling two stitches together. When shaping garments, decreasings are usually worked on a right-side row but if necessary can also be made on a wrong-side row.

Right-sloping decreases

Knitting two stitches together (abbreviated as k2tog)
This form of decrease will slope stitches from left to right on a right-side row.

1 Insert the tip of the right needle knitwise (from left to right) up into the next two stitches on the left needle.

2 Knit these two stitches together as if they were one stitch.

Purling two stitches together (abbreviated as p2tog)
Shown worked at the beginning of a wrong-side row.

This decrease will also slope stitches from left to right when viewed from the right side. It looks the same as k2tog, but is worked on a wrong-side row.

1 Insert the tip of the right needle purlwise (from right to left) through the next two stitches on the left needle.

2 Purl the two stitches together as if they were one stitch.

Left-sloping decreases

Slip 1, knit one, pass slip stitch over (abbreviated as sl1, k1, psso)
Shown worked on the last two stitches of a right-side row.

1 Insert the tip of the right needle knitwise (from left to right) into the next stitch on the left needle. Slip the stitch onto the right-hand needle, without working it (sl1).

2 Knit the next stitch in the usual way (k1).

3 Insert the tip of the left needle into the slipped stitch.

4 Lift the slipped stitch over the knitted stitch and off the needle, as when binding off (psso). One stitch has now been decreased. This decrease slopes from the right to the left when viewed from the right side.

Purl two together through back of loops (abbreviated as p2tog tbl)
Shown worked on the last two stitches of a wrong-side row. This decrease also produces a slope from right to left when viewed from the right side of the work.

1 On a purl row, insert the tip of the right needle from the back of the work, left to right through the next two stitches on the left needle.

2 Purl the two stitches together as if they were one stitch.

CHUNKY KNITS

Gauge

The gauge of a piece of knitting is the number of stitches and the number of rows counted over a certain measurement, usually 4 in. (10 cm), and over a stated stitch pattern. Patterns give a recommended gauge, which must be followed for successful results. If you do not work to the correct gauge, the knitting will end up the wrong size. Although a pattern will give a specific needle size for the yarn to be used, it is given as a guide and a slightly different needle size may need to be used to achieve the desired gauge.

It is necessary to knit up a test swatch in order to check your gauge before you start on the actual garment. Using the yarn that you have chosen for your knitted item, and the specified needle size, cast on a few more stitches than the amount given over 4 in. (10 cm). Make sure that you cast on a suitable number of stitches to work the repeat of the stitch pattern. Work a few more rows than the number given in the instructions as the edge stitches are likely to become distorted. If necessary, block the test piece as instructed for the finished item.

1 Lay the test piece right-side up on a flat surface and use a tape measure or ruler to measure exactly 4 in. (10 cm) along a straight row of stitches across the middle of the swatch. Mark this distance with two pins. Count the number of stitches between the pins, including any part stitches. This is the number of stitches over 4 in. (10 cm).

2 Now, in the same way, measure 4 in. (10 cm) down a vertical column of stitches in the center of the piece. Count the number of rows between the pins. This is the number of rows over 4 in. (10 cm). For some stitch structures, you may find it easier to count rows on the wrong side of the swatch.

Substituting yarn

You can follow a pattern with any yarn if it will knit to the correct gauge. If you are planning to use a different yarn to that specified, look at the ball band information and try to match the recommended gauge and needle size as closely as possible to the pattern. If you are in any doubt, buy just one ball and check the gauge can be matched before you buy the full amount of yarn needed.

Finishing and Sewing Up

Most knitted fabrics need to be blocked before they are stitched together. This is the process of pinning and then fixing the pieces to the correct size and shape. This also helps to even out stitches and to stop edges from curling up, thereby making them easier to sew together. Some stitch structures or parts of garment are best left unpressed—for example, ribbed trims, cable, and textural details.

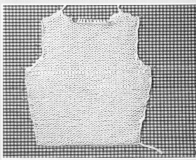

Blocking
You will need a flat surface on which to pin out your knitted pieces. An ironing board is suitable for smaller pieces, but larger pieces will need to be pinned to a blocking board. A checked fabric will help you to lay the work straight. Lay the knitted piece wrong-side up on the blocking board and pin it to shape, keeping the rows and stitches straight. Place pins at right angles to the edge around the edges to be blocked.

Wet spray method
Suitable for textured surfaces and for synthetic and fluffy yarns that should not be pressed or steamed. Use a water spray to dampen the fabric thoroughly, making sure that the moisture penetrates right through the fabric by patting gently with your hand or a damp cloth. Leave the work pinned to the board until it is completely dry.

Steam method
You can use a steam iron for textured or flat fabrics, or a damp cotton cloth and a warm iron for flat fabrics, in order to steam the pieces to shape. If using a steam iron, hold it close to the surface of the fabric, but do not let it touch. Move the iron slowly and evenly over the fabric until it is completely damp from steam and then leave to dry before unpinning. If using a damp cloth, cover the pinned out piece with a damp pressing cloth and press lightly and evenly without dragging the iron over the fabric. When all the fabric has been steamed, leave to dry before removing the pins.

Weaving in yarn ends
Yarn ends are left whenever you change color, join a new ball, or sew up seams. Make sure that the tails of yarn left are about 6 in. (15 cm) long so that they can be easily threaded into a tapestry needle and woven into the back of the work. Avoid tying ends with knots as they can work loose or move through to the front of the fabric.

Weaving in along a row
1 Undo any knots joining yarns before weaving in. Thread the tail of yarn into a tapestry needle and weave it in and out of the back of stitches of the same color, working along a row for about four to six stitches.

Weaving in along a seam
Yarn ends can be run in along the edge of knitting, along the seam. Thread the tail of yarn into a tapestry needle and run the needle in and out of the stitches inside the seam at the edge of the knitting for about 2½ or 3 in. (6 or 8 cm). Pull the yarn through and trim the end.

2 Take the needle back, catching into the woven-in yarn end for a couple of stitches to secure the end. Stretch the knitting widthways and trim the end.

Mattress stitch seam—joining two edges

Seams are ideally sewn in the same yarn that was used to knit the garment, but if this is very textured or weak, it may be necessary to use a finer, smoother yarn in a matching color. It is not advisable to use the tails of yarn left from knitting the garment when sewing up, because if you make a mistake and a seam needs to be undone you may accidentally cut into the knitting. Always use a blunt-ended tapestry or darning needle in a size suitable for the yarn. Mattress stitch is ideal when joining the edges of most types of knitting, when the two pieces to be joined have identical numbers of rows. This seam can be worked one whole or half a stitch in from the edge, depending on the weight of yarn used. Most chunky yarns should be seamed half a stitch in, to avoid bulk; for less chunky yarns, follow the same procedure, but work a whole stitch in from the edge. Mattress stitch creates a neat seam that is almost invisible from the right side.

1 Lay the pieces to be joined flat, side by side with right sides facing you. Leave the yarn end at the back of the fabric to be woven in later. Bring the needle through to the front in the middle of the first stitch (or between the first two stitches) on the first row of the seam.

2 Insert the needle from the right side into the middle of the first stitch on the other piece of fabric to be joined and bring it out in the middle of the edge stitch one row up.

3 Insert the needle back into the first piece of fabric, from the right side in the same place that the yarn last came through on that edge. Bring the needle out a row above that point.

4 Repeat this process, making a zigzag from edge to edge, for a few rows.

5 Pull the yarn through to tighten the seam, holding the tail end securely and continue with the seam. The seam should appear invisible from the right side. When it is finished, weave in the loose ends of yarn to secure and neaten.

Mattress stitch seam—
joining stitches to rows

Mattress stitch is also useful when joining a bound-off edge to a side edge, for example, when joining a sleeve to an armhole. The number of stitches and the number of rows to be joined will not match exactly, therefore it may be advisable to pin the seam before stitching or to start the seam at the center point and work along one direction at a time.

1 Lay the two pieces flat, edge to edge. Leave the yarn end at the back of the fabric to be woven in later. Bring the needle through to the front in the middle of the first stitch of the bound-off edge. Insert the needle in the middle of the first stitch of the row opposite and bring it out again one row above that point.

2 Insert the needle back into the center of the same stitch of the bound-off edge and bring it back through at the center of the next stitch along.

3 Repeat this process for a few stitches, making a zigzag, occasionally compensating for the different amount of stitches and rows by picking up two strands at a time from the edge of the knitting.

4 Pull the yarn to tighten the seam, which should be invisible from the right side. Work along the length of the seam in this way. When it is finished, weave in the loose ends of yarn to secure and neaten.

Backstitch seam

Many patterns recommend backstitch to join seams, although it is not often suitable for chunky weight yarns as it can create bulk. It creates a strong, firm join and can be useful at the shoulder seam and also when sewing zippers into place.

1 Lay the pieces to be joined flat, and pin with edges matching and right sides facing. Insert the needle up between the first and second stitches of both pieces, leaving a tail of yarn at the back. Take the needle around the edge and insert it in the same place to make a strong first stitch.

2 Take the needle around the side edge again and bring through to the front, one knitted stitch along from the first stitch.

3 Insert the needle into the fabric just behind where the first stitch ended, take it along the back of the work for two stitches, and bring through to the front.

4 Repeat step 3, working along the seam. Weave in the yarn end and tail to neaten.

CHUNKY

KNIT PROJECTS

CHUNKY KNITS

PROJECT 1: Woolly Winter Scarf

This warm, chunky scarf follows the current catwalk style: long, ribbed, and stripy with deep pocket detailing. A perfect starter project, you can knit your way from start to finish while curled up in front of your favorite TV program, and stun your friends the next morning. Now you've proved you can knit!

Materials

131 yds (120 m) super chunky slubby wool yarn—color A
175 yds (160 m) super chunky wool yarn—color B
Smooth chunky yarn for contrast oversewing
1 pair size 19 (15 mm) needles
Tapestry needle
A few safety pins

Gauge

Over double rib on size 19 (15 mm) needles: 8–9 sts and 9–10 rows to 4 in. (10 cm)

Finished measurements

Approx 8 in. (20 cm) x 48 in. (160 cm), with pockets sewn up.

Abbreviations

k–knit; **p**–purl; **st(s)**–stitch(es)

To knit the scarf

Cast on 18 sts in yarn A and size 19 (15 mm) needles, using the cable cast on method.
The scarf is worked in double rib throughout.
Row 1 K2, (p2, k2) to end.
This means knit the first two stitches, then purl two stitches and knit two stitches to the end of the row. (You will knit the last two stitches.)
Row 2 P2, (k2, p2) to end.
This means purl the first two stitches, then knit two stitches and purl two stitches to the end of the row.
Repeat rows 1 and 2 to knit double rib for the length of the scarf.
Continue in color A until you have knitted 4 rows.

Stripe Pattern

Instructions for joining new yarn are given on page 21.

Row 5 Change color to create the stripe pattern as follows:
4 rows color B
2 rows color A
4 rows color B
4 rows color A

Repeat the 14-row stripe pattern another 12 times, so ending with a final stripe of 4 rows in color A. You will have knitted 186 rows and the scarf should measure about 75 in. (190 cm). Bind off ribwise in yarn A (page 22).

Finishing

Sew in all ends, following the instructions
on page 36.

Pockets

Fold the scarf 18 rows from both ends,
to make the deep pockets.
Use safety pins to hold in place.
Using a contrast-color chunky yarn,
start at the bottom corner and
oversew the pockets in place,
stitching on the right side so
that the oversewing is visible.
(See page 37.)

Weaving in Loose Ends

Loose ends are ideally hidden on the wrong side of a fabric, but a scarf needs to look good on both sides. When working with very chunky yarn, the loose ends can be difficult to conceal without creating bulk. For this ribbed scarf they are best hidden on the purl side of the stitches. Always weave loose ends into knitting of the same color.

1 Thread the loose end of the yarn into a large-eyed tapestry needle, and weave in and out of two like-color edge stitches on the purl side of the rib.

2 Pass the needle through the purl side of two stitches along the row, and pull the thread through.

3 Double back, stitching into the yarn of the woven-in end, splitting the thread. This will stop the end from working loose.

4 Pull gently to stretch the knitting so that the woven-in yarn is not stitched too tightly into place, or this may distort the fabric.

5 Trim the end of the yarn and repeat the process with all loose ends.

Oversewing Pockets into Position

Oversewing can be used as a decorative way of seaming and finishing edges of knitted fabric. Choose a similar weight yarn in a contrast or matching color. Avoid using very slubby or uneven yarns, which can be difficult to work with.

1 Pin the knitting to position, wrong sides together, matching edges. With very chunky yarn it is often easier to use safety pins, as dressmaker's pins can slip through the fabric. Starting at the bottom corner, make sure that the knot is on the inside of the pocket and stitch through to the front of the knitting.

2 Take the yarn over the edge to the back of the scarf, two rows along and stitch through both layers to the front. Repeat this action, moving another two rows along the seam with each stitch. Pull the yarn so that the stitches wrap firmly over the edge of the seam, holding it into place.

3 Work along the seam in this way until you get to the top corner of the pocket

4 Stitch once again over the corner stitch making a double stitch. Pull the yarn to tighten this stitch and strengthen at this point. Overstitch in the same way along the single layer across the top of the pocket and make another double stitch at the other corner before working down the opposite side of the pocket. Turn the pocket inside out to secure the end on the wrong side.

CHUNKY KNITS

PROJECT 2: Hippie Shoulder Bag

This low-slung bag is a chunky update of bohemian hippie chic. Experiment with easy detailing like the pouch pocket and buttonhole tab or tie fastenings to complete the look. Simple decreasing techniques are used to make the roomy shape.

Materials
310 yds (280 m) super chunky wool mix yarn
Toggle or button
1 pair size 11 (8 mm) needles
1 pair size 15 (10 mm) needles
Large-eyed tapestry needle

Gauge
Over stockinette stitch on size 15 (10 mm) needles:
9 sts and 12 rows to 4 in. (10 cm)

Finished measurements
Width 18 in. (46 cm)
Depth 12 ½ in. (32 cm)

Abbreviations
k–knit; **p**–purl; **st(s)**–stitch(es); **rs**–right side; **ws**–wrong side; **k2tog**–knit two stitches together; **p2tog**–purl two stitches together; **yf**–bring yarn forward to make a yarn over

To knit bag
Front piece
Using size 11 (8 mm) needles, cast on 42 sts.

Rib top edge
Work double rib as follows:
Row 1 (K2, p2) to last 2 sts, k2.
Row 2 (P2, k2) to last 2 sts, p2.
Repeat these 2 rows three more times to row 8.

Main body of bag
Stockinette stitch as follows:
Change empty size 11 (8 mm) needle for a size 15 (10 mm) needle.
Row 9 With rs facing you, knit all stitches.
Change other empty size 11 (8 mm) needle for a size 15 (10 mm) needle.
Row 10 With ws facing you, purl all sts.

Using size 15 (10 mm) needles, continue to work these two rows to row 33.

Bottom shaping
Row 34 (Ws facing) P2, *(p2tog, p1), repeat from * to last stitch, purl last st.
You will now have decreased 13 sts and have 29 sts left on the needle.
Row 35 K.
Row 36 P.
Row 37 K.
Row 38 P.
Row 39 K.
Row 40 P.
Bind off all stitches.

Back piece
Repeat pattern for front.

Pocket
Rib top edge
Cast on 14 sts on size 11 (8 mm) needles.
Work 8 rows in double rib as rows 1 and 2 of front.

Stockinette stitch
Row 9 Change to size 15 (10 mm) needle as for front. Knit all stitches.
Row 10 Change to other size 15 (10 mm) needle. Purl all stitches.
Continue in stockinette stitch on size 15 (10 mm) needles to row 19.
Row 20 (Ws facing) P1, *(p2tog, p1), repeat from * three more times, purl last stitch.
You now have 10 stitches.
Row 21 K.
Row 22 P.

Bind off all stitches.

Straps

Make two alike.

Cast on 5 stitches on size 15 (10 mm)
   needles.

Work 100 rows in stockinette stitch.

Bind off.

Tab

Cast on 7 sts on size 15 (10 mm) needles.

Row 1 K1, p1, k3, p1, k1.

Row 2 P1, k1, p3, k1, p1.

Repeat these two rows to row 16.

Eyelet button hole

Row 17 K1, p1, k1, yf, k2tog, p1, k1.

You should still have 7 stitches on your needle.

Row 18 P1, k1, p3, k1, p1.

Row 19 K1, p1, k3, p1, k1.

Row 20 P1, k1, p3, k1, p1.

Shaping the tip

Row 21 K2tog, k3, k2tog – 5 sts.

Row 22 P2tog, p1, p2tog = 3 sts.

Bind off all 3 stitches.

Assembly

The rib edges will form the opening at
   the top of the bag.

Pin the pocket into position on the front
   of the bag with the rib at the top,
   making sure that it is centered. Stitch into
   place using oversewing, leaving the top open.

Join back and front pieces along the side and
   bottom seams using mattress stitch.

Find the center front and count four stitches along
   to the left and then the right on the first row of
   stockinette stitch. Mark these points with pins.
   Position the ends of one strap either side of the
   markers. Making sure that it is not twisted, pin
   the ends of the strap into place, covering the rib.

Stitch the ends neatly into place with backstitch.

Repeat for the other strap on the back piece.

Lay the bag flat, with the back facing you. Pin the
   flat end of the tab onto the center of the bag,
   covering the rib, and the pointed end protruding
   past the edge with the right sides toward you.
   Stitch into place from the right side, working
   with backstitch.

Turn the bag over and let
   the tab fold over into place.

Mark the position for a button or toggle to line up
   with the eyelet and stitch into place on the front.
   (Make sure that the button fits through the hole
   before sewing.)

CHUNKY KNITS

Making an Eyelet Hole

The yarnover technique is the most useful way of making a hole in knitting. When working with chunky yarn, an eyelet is usually big enough to be used as a buttonhole or for threading with ties. Always check that the button to be used is a suitable size. This yarnover hole is actually an increase worked between two knit stitches on the right side of your knitting. It is called "yarn forward" and abbreviated on knitting patterns as yf. The yarn forward is usually accompanied by a decrease so that you are left with the correct amount of stitches at the end of the row. In this example the decrease is "knit two together" (k2tog) directly after the yarnover has been made. The same yarnover method can also be used to create decorative holes in lace knitting.

1 On a knit row, work to the point where you wish to make an eyelet

2 Bring the yarn forward between the two needles. This makes the yarnover hole.

3 Knit the next two stitches together (k2tog), taking the yarn round the back of the right needle to do so.

4 Work to the end of the row and on the next row treat the yarnover as a stitch.

5 You should still have the same amount of stitches on your needles.

Tab with Crochet Tie

As an alternative to the eyelet buttonhole tab, you can work a pair of tabs with ties. The ties are crocheted using a crochet hook large enough for your yarn. Crochet techniques are often used when trimming knitwear.

Cast on 5 stitches.
Work 6 rows in stockinette stitch, starting with a knit row.
Next row K2tog, k1, k2tog = 3 sts.
Work 1 row purl.
Bind off both edge stitches over center stitch as follows:

1 Slip 1, k1, pass slip stitch over.

2 Turn work and slip worked stitch onto right needle with other stitch.

3 Lift bottom stitch over worked stitch.

4 Cut the yarn leaving a 12 in. (30 cm) tail and slip remaining stitch onto a crochet hook.

Crocheting a chain for length of tie

1 Hold yarn coming from tab taut in one hand and the hook in other hand.

2 Pass the hook under then over the yarn and pull through the stitch, making a new chain stitch on the hook.

3 Repeat for length of chain, leaving a 2 in. (5 cm) tail.

4 Fasten off by pulling the end through the last chain stitch.

5 Use the hook to weave in the loose end, working back along the chain, stitch by stitch.

The tabs should be sewn to position as for the eyelet tab on both center back and front of the bag so that the ties meet at the top.

CHUNKY KNITS

PROJECT 3: Man's Raglan Rollover

Large and masculine, this stripy raglan is relaxed and sporty. The deep rollover turtle-neck, cuffs, and hem are all knitted in chunky ribs. Knit for the love in your life without making a labor of love! Or scale down the sleeve length to produce a favorite baggy sweater for your own wardrobe!

Materials

Extra-chunky machine-washable wool mix:
Color A—492(575, 646) yds [450(560, 650) m]
Color B—328(350, 365) yds [300(320, 335) m]
1 pair size 11 (8 mm) needles
1 pair size 10½ (7 mm) needles for rib
4 stitch holders
Tapestry needle

Gauge

Over stockinette stitch on size 11 (8 mm)
   needles: 12 sts and 16 rows to 4 in. (10 cm)

Finished measurements

Actual chest measurement 43½(46, 48) in.
   [110(117, 122) cm]
Center back length 27½(31, 33½ in).
   [70(78, 85) cm]
Longer sleeve seam 20½ in. (52 cm); shorter
   sleeve seam 18½ in. (47 cm). Cuff folded for
   all sizes

Abbreviations

st(s)–stitch(es); **k**–knit; **p**–purl; **rs**–right side;
st.st–stockinette stitch; **sl1, k1, psso**–slip 1,
knit 1, pass slip stitch over; **k2tog**–knit 2
stitches together; **p2tog**–purl 2 stitches
together

Back

Double rib

Using color A, cast on 66(74, 82) sts on size
10½ (7 mm) needles.
Row 1 K2, (p2, k2) to end of row.
Row 2 P2, (k2, p2) to end of row.
Repeat until you have worked 12 rows.

Stockinette stitch

Change to size 11
(8 mm) needles
still working in color A.
With rs facing work in st.st:
Row 1 K.
Row 2 P.

Stripes

Row 3 Change to color B and work 10 rows
   in st.st.
Change to color A and change color for stripe
   every 10 rows from now on.
Continue to work striped stockinette stitch for
   60 rows, ending with a purl row.

Raglan armhole shaping

Underarm shaping

With rs facing, bind off 3 sts, knit to end
   of row.
Bind off 3 sts, purl to end of row =
   60(68, 76) sts.

Decreasing for raglan

(Change color to B.)
Decrease at beginning and end of all knit rows
   as follows:
Row 1 K1, sl1, k1, psso, k to last 3 sts,
   k2tog, k1.
Row 2 P.
Repeat rows 1 and 2 to row 40(44, 48), leaving
   20(22, 24) stitches while at the same time
   continue striping every 10 rows: (row 11
   change to A, row 21 to B, row 31 to A, row
   41 to B). Put all stitches onto stitch holder.
   The stitches will be picked up for the
   neckband. (See page 46.)

Front

Work as for Back to row 34(38, 42) of decreasing.

Front neck shaping

First side

(Rs facing, 26(30, 34) sts on needle.)

Row 35(39, 43) K1, sl1, k1, psso, k6(7, 8) and work on these 8(9, 10) sts.

Put remaining 17(20, 23) stitches onto stitch holder.

Row 36(40, 44) P2tog, p6(7, 8).

Row 37(41, 45) K1, sl1, k1, psso, k2(3, 4), k2tog.

Row 38(42, 46) P2tog, p3(4, 5).

Row 39(43, 47) K2tog, k0(1, 2), k2tog.

Row 40(44, 48) P2tog, p0(1, 2)

Second size only. **Row 45** K2tog.

Third size only. **Row 49** K3tog.

Bind off remaining stitch.

Second side

With rs facing, working on remaining 17(20, 23) stitches, slip 8(10, 12) center front stitches onto stitch holder; these stitches will be picked up when you knit the neckband.

Rejoin yarn to remaining 9(10, 11) stitches.

Row 35(39, 43) K6(7, 8), k2tog, k1.

Row 36(40, 44) P6(7, 8), p2tog.

Row 37(41, 45) K2tog, k2(3, 4), k2tog, k1.

Row 38(42, 46) P3(4, 5), p2tog.

Row 39(43, 47) K2tog, k0(1, 2), k2tog.

Row 40(44, 48) P0(1, 2), p2tog.
Second size only. **Row 45** K2tog.
Third size only. **Row 49** K3tog.
Bind off remaining stitch.

Sleeves (knit two)
Ribbed cuffs
On size 10½ (7 mm) needles, cast on 30(34, 38)
    sts in color A.
Row 1 K2, (p2, k2) rib to end of row.
Row 2 P2, (k2, p2) to end of row.
Repeat these 2 rows until you have
    20(20, 20) rows or 16(16,16) rows for
    shorter sleeve length.

Stockinette stitch
With rs facing, work on size 11 (8 mm) needles
    in color A.
For shorter sleeve length start on row 5 of
    stockinette stitch.
Working in stockinette stitch:
Row 1 K. (Start here for longer sleeve length.)
Row 2 P.
Row 3 K.
Row 4 P.
Row 5 (Start here for shorter sleeve length.
)Increase 1 st on first and last st of
    row = 32(34, 38) sts.
Row 6 P.
Row 7 Change to color B. Knit.
Continue working in st.st, increasing as for row
    5 at the beginning and end of every 6th row,
    and from now on change color every 10 rows
    as follows:
Row 11 Increase.
Row 17 Change color to A and increase.
Row 23 Increase.
Row 27 Change color to B.
Rows 29 and 35 Increase.
Row 37 Change color to A.
Row 41 Increase.
Row 47 Change color to B and increase.
Row 53 Increase.
You now have 48(53, 56) stitches.

Continue working all stitches for 3 more rows.
Row 57 Change to color A. Continue working
    all stitches for 8 rows, to row 64.

Sleeve underarm shaping
(Rs facing.)
Row 1 Bind off 3 sts, k to end of row.
Row 2 Bind off 3 sts, p to end of row.
You have 42(46, 50) stitches.

Shaping for raglan
Change color to B.
Decrease at beginning and end of all knit rows
    as follows:
Row 1 K1, sl1, k1, psso, k to last 3 sts,
    k2tog, k1.
Row 2 Purl all stitches.
Repeat rows 1 and 2 to row 24. (Change color
    at rows 11 and 21.)
Work 2 rows without decreasing.
You have 18(22, 26) sts.
Row 27 Decrease 1 stitch at both ends, as
    for row 1 = 16(20, 24) sts.
Work 2 rows without decreasing.
Row 30 P.
Row 31 Change to color A. Knit.
Row 32 P.
Row 33 Decrease 1 stitch at both ends of row
    as for row 1 = 14(18, 22) sts.
Work 14 remaining sts in st.st for 7 rows
    to row 40.
First size only. Put 14 stitches onto stitch
    holder, these stitches will be picked up for
    the neckband.
Second size and third sizes only. **Row 41**
    Change to color B. Decrease 1 stitch at both
    ends of row as for row 1 = (16, 20) sts.
Row 42 P.
Row 43 K.
Row 44 P
Second size only. Put 16 stitches onto stitch
    holder, these stitches will be picked up for
    the neckband.
Third size only. **Row 45** Decrease 1 stitch of
    row as for row 1 = (18) sts.
Row 46 P.
Row 47 K.

Row 48 P.

Put 18 stitches onto stitch holder, these stitches
will be picked up for the neckband.

Finishing
Neckband

Block and steam all pieces (see page 29).

Join 3 raglan seams, using mattress stitch, working
one stitch in, leaving left back raglan seam open.

Picking up stitches

(See page 47.)

Work in color A, with rs facing, using size 10½ (7)
mm needles, starting with stitches on a stitch
holder at top of left sleeve, working toward front.

Knit 14(16, 18) sts from stitch holder at top of
left sleeve.

Knit 5(5, 5) sts evenly along left side of
neck shaping.

Knit 8(10, 12) sts at front of neck.

Knit 5(5, 5) sts evenly along right side of
neck shaping.

Knit 14(16, 18) sts on stitch holder at top of
right sleeve.

Knit 20(22, 24) sts left on stitch holder on
back of neck.

You now have 66(78, 90) sts on the needles.

Work neckband in double rib for 29 rows, starting
first row with p2, k2.

Bind off loosely ribwise.

Assembly

Use mattress stitch, in color A.

Match stripes carefully; this is easy to do in
mattress stitch as you are working from
the right side.

Join raglan seams.

Join neckband seam, reversing seam halfway up,
for fold over (see page 47).

Join side and underarm seams, reversing seam
halfway on rib cuffs for fold over.

Holding and Picking up Stitches

Stitches on the needle can be slipped onto a holder without being bound off. The stitches are left open to be picked up and knitted at a later stage. This technique is often used around a neckline, when a collar is to be knitted on. If only a small amount of stitches are to be put on a holder, you could use a large safety pin instead. Be careful not to split the yarn with the pointed end of the holder.

To slip stitches onto a stitch holder

1 Hold the needle with the stitches in your left hand. Insert the tip of the stitch holder up into the middle of the first stitch on the needle from right to left and slip the stitch from the left needle onto the holder.

2 Work along the row of stitches, one by one in this way. When the correct number of stitches are on the holder, fasten it and continue following the pattern.

Picking up stitches from a stitch holder

1 Hold the stitch holder in your left hand. With the needle in your right hand, insert the tip into the middle of the first stitch and slip the stitch from the holder to the right needle.

2 Work along the row of stitches, one by one like this. When all the stitches are on the needle, put the needle in your left hand and continue following the pattern.

Picking up stitches from the edge of knitting

This useful method is used to knit onto bound-off, shaped, or side edges of knitting, such as shaping on a neckline, or knitting a band onto an opening. It is important to work accurately from your pattern, working the required number of stitches. This picking up row is also referred to as knitting up, as it creates a row of knit stitches on your needle.

1 Hold the knitting in your left hand with the right side facing you. Hold the needle in your right hand, with the yarn at the back. Starting at the first right-hand stitch to be picked up, push the needle through the knitting from front to back, one stitch in from the edge.

2 Wrap the yarn around the needle and pull the loop through the edge stitch, just like knitting a plain stitch.

3 Knit into the next stitch to the left in the same way and continue to knit into the edge of the knitting, working from right to left until you have picked up the correct amount of stitches onto the needle.

Sewing Ribs on Fold-over Cuff and Neckbands

For fold-over cuffs and collar, the seams need to be reversed halfway along for a neat finish. Mattress stitch is fully explained in on page 30. When sewing double rib in mattress stitch, work one stitch in from the edge as usual. If sewing single rib or with super chunky yarns, it is neater to work only a half stitch in from the edge.

1 With the wrong side facing you, starting at the bottom edge of the rib, work in mattress stitch up to halfway along the seam, and pull to tighten the last stitch.

2 Turn the work so that the right sides are facing you and bring the needle over the edge of the fabric to the right side of the work. Pass the needle into the right side of the opposite edge to make the next stitch.

3 Continue to work in mattress stitch along the seam, now working from the right side.

CHUNKY

KNITS

PROJECT 4: Ladies' Turtleneck Raglan

This is a narrow fitting, fully-fashioned raglan sweater with a distinctive, slouchy, garter stitch turtleneck. Using very little knitting know-how, this silhouette can be adapted to create a crop top or a longline sweater. Experiment with an offbeat, laddered raglan detail.

Materials

480(525, 570, 620) yds [440(480, 525, 570) m]
  super chunky wool yarn
1 pair size 19 (15 mm) needles
Large tapestry needle

Gauge

Over stockinette stitch on size 19 (15 mm needles):
  7½ sts and 10 rows to 4 in. (10 cm)

Finished measurements

Center back length 21½ (22½, 23¼, 24) in.
  [55(57, 59, 61) cm]
*Cropped sweater 18(19, 19½, 20½) in.
  [46(48, 50, 52) cm]
**Longline sweater 25½ (26½, 27, 28) in.
  [65(67, 69, 71) cm]
Bust measurement 36(38, 40, 42) in.
  [91(96, 102, 107)cm]
Sleeve seam 16½ in. (42 cm) for all sizes.

Abbreviations

k–knit; **p**–purl; **st.st**–stockinette stitch; **st(s)**–stitch(es); **rh**–right hand; **tog**–together; **k2tog**–knit two stitches together; **p2tog**–purl two stitches together; **sl**–slip; **psso**–pass slip stitch over; **sl1, k1, psso**–slip 1, knit 1, pass slip stitch over; **yf**–bring yarn forward to make a yarn over

Back

Cast on 36(38, 40, 42) stitches.
Row 1 K.
Row 2 P.
Continue working in st.st to row 33 (*25, **45).

*If you require a cropped shape, stop knitting at row 25 and then continue with pattern from row 34.
**If you require a longline sweater, knit 12 extra rows at this point (= 45 rows) and then continue with pattern from row 34.

Shaping for raglan

Row 34 Bind off 2 sts, p to end.
Row 35 Bind off 2 sts, k2 (you will have 3 sts on rh needle), sl1, k1, psso, k to last 5 stitches, k2tog, k3 = 30(32, 34, 36) sts.
Row 36 P.
Row 37 K3, sl1, k1, psso, k to last 5 sts, k2tog, k3 = 28 (30, 32, 34) sts.
Row 38 P to end.

Repeat rows 37 and 38 to row 50(52, 54, 56)
  = 16 sts.
Row 51(53, 55, 57) K3, sl1, k1, psso, k to last 5 sts, k2tog, k3 = 14 sts.
Row 52(54, 56, 58) P.
Row 53(55, 57, 59) K.
Row 54(56, 58, 60) P.
Bind off loosely.

Front

Cast on 36(38, 40, 42) sts and work as Back to row 33 (*25, **45).

*If you require a cropped shape, stop knitting at row 25 and then continue with pattern from row 34.
**If you require a longline sweater, knit 12 extra rows at this point (= 45 rows) and then continue with pattern from row 34.

Continue to work as Back to row 50(52, 54, 56)
  = 16 sts.

Left neck

Row 51(53, 55, 57) K3, sl1, k1, psso and work on these 4 sts. Put remaining 11 stitches on stitch holder.
Row 52(54, 56, 58) P all 4 sts.
Row 53(55, 57, 59) K2tog, k2tog (2 sts remain).
Row 54(56, 58, 60) P2tog, fasten off (break yarn and thread through loop).

Right neck

Put 11 sts back onto needle and rejoin
yarn. (Rs facing.)

Row 51(53, 55, 57) Bind off 5 sts
knitwise loosely for neck, then k next 2 sts
tog on left needle and use stitch to bind off a
6th stitch on right needle. K3.

Row 52(54, 56, 58) P 4 sts.

Row 53(55, 57, 59) K2tog, k2tog.

Row 54(56, 58, 60) P2tog. Fasten off.

Sleeves (knit two)

Cast on 16(18, 20, 22) sts.

Row 1 K.

Row 2 P.

Continue to work in stockinette stitch to row 10.

Increasing

Work increase row as follows:

Row 11 K into front and back of stitch. K to last two
sts, k into front and back of st, knit last st.

Increase as row 11 on every 4th row (rows 15, 19, 23,
27, 31, 35, 39) = 32(34, 36, 38) sts.

Row 40 P.

Making the yarnover holes at bottom
of runs

(This is important to stop the runs running too far.)

Row 41 K3, k2tog, yf, k to last 5 sts, yf, k2tog, k3.

Shaping for raglan

Row 42 Bind off 2 sts purlwise, p to end – 30(32, 34,
36) sts.

Row 43 Bind off 2 stitches knitwise, k2 (3 sts on rh
needle), sl1, k1, psso. K to last 5 sts, k2 tog, k3 =
26(28, 30, 32) sts.

Row 44 P.

Row 45 K3, sl1, k1, psso, K to last 5 sts, k2tog, k3.

Repeat rows 44 and 45 to row 60(62, 64, 66) = 10 sts.

Row 61(63, 65, 67) K3, sl1, k1, psso, k2tog,
k3 = 8 sts.

Dropping stitches to ladder the raglan

(See page 50.)

Row 62(64, 66, 68) P2, drop 1, p2, drop 1, p2 = 6 sts.

Bind off the remaining 6 stitches loosely, knitwise.

Pull ladders to run down to yarnover holes.

It is important to run the ladders completely before
steaming, or the yarn will be kinked.

Finishing and Assembly

Block and steam all pieces.

Join three raglan seams with mattress stitch,
working just a half stitch in from the edge, as the
yarn is so bulky.

Garter stitch collar (sideways knitted
turtleneck).

Cast on 12 stitches.

Knit 62 rows (garter stitch) or until collar fits around
the neck edge without being stretched. Bind
off loosely.

Attaching collar band

(See page 51.)

Use safety pins to pin collar band evenly to neck,
edge to edge. Pin to position at seams. Join collar
band to neck edge, using mattress stitch.

Joining final raglan seam and
collar seam.

Join underarm and side seams with mattress stitch,
working a half stitch in from the edge.

CHUNKY KNITS

Putting Runs into Knitting for Detail

A run or ladder can be used as an easily created detail in knitting. The dropped stitch will run down row by row to the point where that stitch was created or cast on; either to a yarnover hole as in the turtleneck raglan, or to the cast-on row. If you are putting laddering into a garment, remember that the dropped stitch will end up wider than a knitted stitch. Allow for this by counting a run as two stitches when calculating width.

Dropping a stitch to create a run

1 A stitch can be dropped on either a purl or knit row in the same way. Work along the row up to the stitch to be dropped. Do not work into this stitch, push the stitch off the end of the left needle, using your finger or the tip of the right needle. Continue to work along the row, dropping any other stitches to be run in the same way. When working the next row, do not work into the dropped stitches.

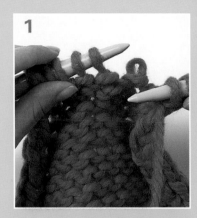

2 When the knitting is bound off, pull the knitting gently either side of the run so that it goes down row by row. If you are working with a very smooth or slippery yarn, the run may go on its own; if your yarn is very textured or slubby, each stitch will need to be pulled separately.

3 It is important to put in the runs completely before blocking, or the strands of yarn will be kinked.

Adding extra detail to a run

You can experiment with decorative detailing by weaving yarns, braids, or strips of leather through the strands of the run.

Attaching Garter Stitch Collar to Body

The side edge of the sideways knitted garter stitch neckband sits flat, overlapping onto the neckline shaping. Garter stitch is very stretchy, so it can easily be eased to fit correctly and evenly. Once the seam has been sewn, the collar can be pulled to the desired shape. The neckband seam and all shoulder seams should be sewn before attaching the collar.

1 Use safety pins to pin the bottom edge of the neck band overlapping the edge over the bound-off row of the neckline, with right sides of both sections facing you.

2 Pass the tapestry needle through to the right side, coming out in the middle of an edge stitch of the collar. Working from right to left, pass the needle under a strand of yarn on the nearest stitch on the main fabric, coming back to the right side.

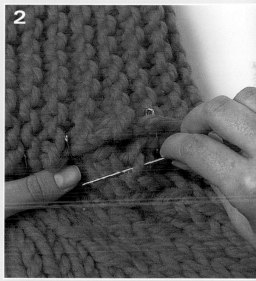

3 Pass the needle through the edge stitch of the collar, two rows along, from wrong side to right side. Continue in this way, working around the neckline

CHUNKY KNITS

PROJECT 5: Chunky Cardigan

This chunky, cozy cardigan is knitted in stockinette stitch with seed stitch detail and buttoned front opening. With inset pockets and a snug collar, this winter essential can be worked as either a jacket or longer coat length.

Materials

Super chunky slubby wool yarn:
Jacket 660(740) yds [600(675) m]
Coat 825(900) yds [750(825) m]
1 pair size 17 (12 mm) needles
4 buttons for jacket, 6 buttons for coat

Gauge

Over seed stitch on size 17 (12 mm) needles:
  8 sts and 12 rows to 4 in. (10 cm)

Finished measurements

Center back length:
Jacket 28(29) in. [71(74) cm]
Coat 38¼(39¼) in. [97(100) cm]
Sleeve length 18(19) in. [46(48) cm]
Bust at underarm 44(48) in. [112(122) cm]

Abbreviations

st(s)–stitch(es); **k**–knit; **p**–purl; **st.st**–stockinette stitch; **beg**–beginning; **sl1, k1, psso**–slip one, knit one, pass slip stitch over; **k2tog**–knit 2 stitches together; **p2tog**–purl 2 stitches together; **rpt**–repeat; **rs**–right side; **ws**–wrong side; **yf**–bring yarn forward; **m1**–make one stitch; **inc**–increase; **tbl**–through back of loops

Back

Using size 17 (12 mm) needles cast on 39(43) stitches.
Work in seed stitch as follows:
Row 1 *(K1, p1) repeat from * to last stitch, k1.

Tip

When working with a hand-dyed yarn, it is advisable to work by alternating two balls at a time in order to disguise color variations between hanks (see page 57).

Work 9 more rows in the same way.
Starting with a knit row, work in st.st until work measures 18 in. (46 cm) x 28½ in. (72 cm).

Armhole shaping

Row 1 Bind off 2 sts at beg row, k to end = 37(41) sts.
Row 2 Bind off 2 sts at beg row, p to end = 35(39) sts.
Row 3 Sl1, k1, psso, k to last 2 sts, k2tog = 33(37) sts.
Row 4 P2tog, p to last 2 sts, p2tog tbl = 31(35) sts.
Row 5 Sl1, k1, psso, k to last 2 sts, k2tog = 29(33) sts.
Starting with a purl row, continue in st.st, until armhole measures 8½ (9½) in. [21.5(24) cm].

Shoulder shaping

Row 1 Bind off 4(5) sts and k to end
Row 2 Bind off 4(5) sts and p to end
Row 3 Bind off 5 sts and k to end
Row 4 Bind off 5 sts and p to end
Put remaining 11(13) stitches onto a stitch holder.

Left front

Using size 17 (12 mm) needles cast on 23(25) sts.
Work 10 rows seed stitch as given for Back.
Row 11 Knit to last 5 sts and work seed st border as follows: k1, p1, k1, p1, k1.
Row 12 Work 5 sts of seed stitch border as follows: k1, p1, k1, p1, k1, and p to end.
Repeat rows 11 and 12 for 6 (38) more rows.

Pocket opening

Row 19(51) Keeping in pattern, work 11(12) sts and slip remaining 12(13) sts onto a stitch holder.

Work outside of opening

Turn work and continue in st.st for 12 more rows ending with a right-side row.

Slip unworked row 18 (50) stitches from inside of opening from stitch holder onto the empty needle.

Slip all worked stitches from outside of opening onto the stitch holder and break yarn.

Work inside of opening

Rejoin yarn to stitches on inside of opening.

Row 19(51) With rs facing, k7(8), work last 5 sts as seed st border.

Row 20(52) Work 5 sts as seed st border, p7(8).

Continue in stockinette stitch with seed stitch border to row 32(64) (ws row).

Do not break yarn.

Close opening

Slip stitches from stitch holder onto empty needle. Hold this needle in your left hand, ws facing.

Row 33(65) Continue in st.st, working across this row in purl = 23(25) sts

Continue working in st.st with seed stitch border until work measures 18 in. (46 cm) x 28 ½ in. (72 cm), ending with a ws row.

Armhole shaping

Continue in st.st with seed st border throughout.

Row 1 Bind off 2 sts, work to end = 21(23) sts.

Row 2 Work to end.

Row 3 Sl1, k1, psso, work to end = 20(22) sts.

Row 4 Work to last 2 sts, p2tog = 19(21) sts.

Row 5 Sl1, k1, psso, work to end = 18(20) sts.

Continue in pattern, starting with a ws row until armhole measures 8½ (9½) in. [21.5 (24) cm].

Shoulder shaping

Row 1 Bind off 4(5) sts and k to end.

Row 2 Work to end.

Row 3 Bind off 5 sts and k to end.

Row 4 Work to end (ws row).

Break yarn and slip 9(10) remaining sts onto a stitch holder for collar.

Right front

Using size 17 (12 mm) needles cast on 25 sts.

Work 10 rows seed stitch as given for Back.

Row 11 Work seed st border with eyelet buttonhole as follows: k1, p1, k2tog, yf, k1, k to end.

Row 12 Purl to last 5 sts, work 5 sts of seed stitch border as follows: k1, p1, k1, p1, k1.

For jacket only

Continue working seed stitch border and st.st to row 18.

Pocket opening

Row 19 Keeping in pattern, work 12(13) sts and slip remaining 11(12) sts onto a stitch holder.

CHUNKY KNITS

For coat only
Continue working seed stitch border and st.st to row 26.

Make eyelet button hole
Row 27 K1, p1, k2tog, yf, k1, work to end.
Continue working seed stitch border and st.st to row 42.

Make eyelet button hole
Row 43 K1, p1, k2tog, yf, k1, work to end.
Continue working seed stitch border and st.st to row 50.

Pocket opening
Row 51 Keeping in pattern, work 12(13) sts and slip remaining 11(12) sts onto a stitch holder.

For both jacket and coat
Work inside of opening
Row 20(52) Turn work and continue in st.st with seed stitch border for 7 more rows = 26 (58) rows.

Make eyelet button hole
Row 27(59) K1, p1, k2tog, yf, k1, work to end.
Continue in pattern to row 31 (63).
Slip unworked row 18 (50) stitches from outside of opening from stitch holder onto the empty needle.
Break yarn and slip all worked stitches from inside of opening onto the stitch holder.

Work outside of opening
Rejoin yarn to stitches on outside of opening.
Row 19(51) With rs facing, work all sts in pattern.
Continue in stockinette stitch to row 32 (64) (ws row).
Do not break yarn.

Close opening
Slip stitches from stitch holder onto empty needle. Hold this needle in your left hand (ws facing).
Row 33(65) Continue in pattern, working across this row = 23(25) sts.
Continue in pattern (st.st with seed stitch border) for 9 more rows to row 42 (74).

Make eyelet button hole
Row 43(75) K1, p1, k2tog, yf, k1, work to end.

*Continue in pattern until work measures 18 in. (46 cm) x 28½ in. (72 cm), ending with a rs row.
(Count rows worked from * after buttonhole in order to position top buttonhole correctly.)

Armhole shaping
Work in st.st with seed st border throughout.
Row 1 Bind off 2 sts, work to end = 21(23) sts.
Row 2 Work to last 2 sts, k2tog = 20(22) sts.
Row 3 Sl1, p1, psso, work to end = 19(21) sts.
Row 4 Work to last 2 sts, k2tog = 18(20) sts.
Continue in pattern, starting with a ws row until a total of 16 rows have been worked from *.

Make top eyelet button hole
Next row K1, p1, k2tog, yf, k1, work to end.
Continue in pattern until armhole measures 8½(9½) in. [21.5(24) cm], ending with a ws row.

Shoulder shaping
Row 1 Work all sts.
Row 2 Bind off 4(5) sts and work to end = 14(15) sts.
Row 3 Work to end.
Row 4 Bind off 5 sts and work to end (ws row) = 9(10) sts.
Break yarn and slip 9(10) remaining sts onto a stitch holder for collar.

Sleeves (knit two)
Using size 17 (12 mm) needles cast on 19(23) sts.
Work 10 rows seed st.
Continue in st.st throughout.

Increasing
Row 15 Inc 1 stitch at beg and end of row = 21(25) sts.
Row 19 Inc 1 stitch at beg and end of row = 23(27) sts.
Row 23 Inc 1 stitch at beg and end of row = 25(29) sts.
Row 27 Inc 1 stitch at beg and end of row = 27(31) sts.
Row 33 Inc 1 stitch at beg and end of row = 29(33) sts.
Row 39 Inc 1 stitch at beg and end of row = 31(35) sts.
Continue in st.st until work measures 18(19) in. [46(48) cm] ending on a ws row.

Sleeve-head shaping
Bind off 3 sts at the beg of the next 2 rows = 25(29) sts.
Bind off 4(3) sts at the beg of the next 2 rows = 17(23) sts.
Bind off 0(3) sts at the beg of next 2 rows = 17(17) sts.
Bind off remaining 17 sts.

Pockets
Left pocket lining
With rs facing, turn front and knit up 11 sts along
outside edge of pocket opening, from top to bottom.
Work 10 rows st.st.
Bind off.

Left pocket trim
(See pages 56–57.)
With rs facing, turn front and knit up 13 sts along
inside edge of pocket opening, from
bottom to top.
Work 6 rows seed stitch.
Bind off.
Pass the pocket lining through the
opening to the wrong side of the
front. Slip stitch into place, working
from the wrong side.
Lay the trim flat on the right side and
stitch the side edges into place.
Repeat, reversing direction for right-
side pocket.

Assembly
Sew in loose ends and block all pieces
to shape using steam method.

Collar
Join shoulder seams using mattress
stitch.
Slip all stitches from stitch holders onto a
size 17 (12 mm) needle as follows:
Slip 9(10) sts from right center front to right
shoulder, 11(13) sts across back neck,
9(10) sts from left shoulder to left center front
= 29(33) sts.
Row 1 Starting at left center front, with ws
facing, work first 5 sts in seed st, *(k1, m1),
repeat from * four more times, knit to last 9
sts, ** (m1, k1) rep from ** three more times.
Work last 5 sts in seed st. 38(42) sts.

Make eyelet buttonhole in rib
collar
Row 2 K1, p1, k2tog, yf, k1, * (k2, p2) repeat from
* to last 5 sts. Work last 5 sts in seed st.
Row 3 Work first 5 sts in seed st, * (k2, p2) repeat
from * to last 5 sts. Work last 5 sts in
seed st.

Inset Pocket

The inset pocket is worked by picking up stitches along the slit opening and then stitching the lining and trim into place to finish. This is usually referred to as "Knit up" or "Pick up and knit." The same technique is used to pick up stitches around a neckline (see page 47).

Picking up stitches with super chunky yarn

The pocket lining and pocket trim are worked by picking up stitches along the side edges of the slit opening. However, when using a super chunky yarn, it is necessary to work through the middle of the edge stitch to avoid bulk, rather than a whole stitch in from the edge. The number of stitches to be knitted up will not always correspond to the existing number of stitches or rows along the edge, so make sure that the stitches are picked up evenly along the edge.

1 Use a pin to mark the halfway point along the edge—this will be the middle stitch to be knitted up. When picking up along a longer edge, mark quarter points and divide stitches evenly between points to ensure accuracy. With rs facing and working from right to left along the edge, insert the point of the right-hand needle from front to back into the middle of the first stitch to be picked up. Wind the yarn around the tip of the needle and draw a loop through as if knitting a stitch.

2 Continue along the edge in this way picking up the required amount of stitches.

Stitching pocket to position using slipstitch

When the pocket lining and the seed stitch trim have been knitted, they must be stitched into place. Slipstitch is used for sewing one piece of knitted fabric on top of another, often for pocket linings or facings. Slipstitch should be worked in the same color yarn as the knitting, but is shown here in a contrasting yarn for clarity.

1 Working from the wrong side, bring the lining through from the right side of the garment so that the reverse stocking stitch side is facing you. Mark the position of the edges on the main fabric using a contrasting color thread to ensure that the piece is laying straight.

2 Thread a large-eyed needle with a length of matching yarn and secure the end, working from the right-hand end of the seam to be sewn. Take the needle under a strand on the wrong side of the main fabric and then up through a stitch on the edge of the pocket lining.

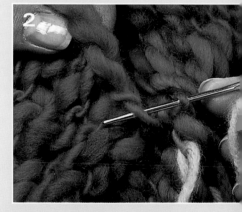

3 Take the needle over the edge of the lining fabric and repeat along the row. It is important that you do not pull the stitches too tightly and that the seam does not show from the right-hand side.

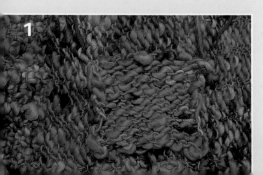

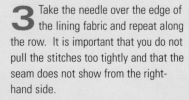

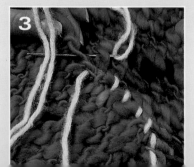

Carrying Yarn Up Side of Work

If using a hand-dyed yarn it is likely that there will be some color variation between hanks of the same color. Therefore, it is advisable to work from two balls at once working stripes of two or four rows from one ball and then two or four rows from the other to obtain an even color effect.

Always change the ball on the seam side so that the opening edges do not become untidy, and carry the yarn up the sides of the work so that there are minimal ends to sew in when finishing.

Sewing on Buttons

A button may be sewn on with a shank to raise it from the fabric if is very bulky or if the edges have a facing. Use a reasonably smooth and strong yarn in the same color as the garment or button.

Use a cable needle or crochet hook as a spacer between the button and the fabric. Stitch the button in place and, when secured, remove the spacer and wind the yarn around the shank a few times. Pass the needle through to the wrong side of the fabric and sew in.

Trimming Selvages

Selvage is the term for the edge stitches of a fabric. Stockinette stitch fabric tends to curl up at the edges and does not always give a neat enough finish for an opening. A border or selvage of moss stitch will lay flat and give a good edge to the opening.

1 The moss stitch borders at the center front openings of the Chunky Cardigan form a simple button and buttonhole band knitted in one with the main fabric as a design feature.

2 The pocket trim is knitted onto the edge of the opening by picking up stitches. Borders can also be added by knitting separately and sewing to a garment.

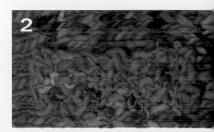

Stitch Techniques

Most knitted fabrics are based on a combination of knit and purl stitches, but many exciting textural effects can be created with a combination of different stitch patterns and techniques. You can try working a stitch pattern in a variety of yarn types and weights to see the different effects produced. Smaller-scale stitch patterns and detailing are generally more defined when worked in smooth yarns and lighter colors, while very tactile surfaces such as poodle loop stitch can be exaggerated with the use of slubby or bouclé yarns. Cable techniques are worked using a special double-pointed cable needle to enable groups of stitches to be crossed over, creating seemingly complex and boldly textured structures and surfaces.

Blackberry popcorn stitch

This is an all-over textured pattern, which is made from a series of raised bobbles (balls of fabric). It is sometimes known as trinity stitch as the pattern is formed with one stitch made from three, then three stitches made from one. The method of knitting several times into one stitch is also often used in Fisherman-style knitting along with cable designs to create individual bobbles. These groups of increases and decreases create a knobbly surface to the knitting. This stitch works well knitted quite loosely to create a more open surface. The first and last stitch of each row are usually worked without pattern, so that the edges of the knitted pieces can be seamed together easily. The instructions for stitch patterns give a guide to the number of stitches needed to work the repeat correctly.

Instructions for blackberry popcorn stitch

Cast on a multiple of 4 sts (+ 2 sts).
Row 1 (Right side) Purl to end.
Row 2 K1, *(k1, p1, k1) all in next st, p3tog, rpt from * to last st, k1.
Row 3 Purl to end.
Row 4 K1, *p3tog, (k1, p1, k1) all in next st, rpt from * to last st, k1.
Repeat.

The instruction "(k1, p1, k1) all in next stitch," means that you are increasing twice into the same stitch, thereby making two new stitches.

1 Knit into the next stitch as usual, but don't let the stitch slip off the needle.

2 Bring the yarn forward and purl into the same stitch, still without letting the stitch slip off the needle.

3 Now take the yarn back again and knit once more into same stitch.

4 This time let the original stitch slip off the needle, completing the stitch. You have now made three stitches from the one original stitch.

The next instruction "p3tog" means that you are decreasing two stitches at once, by purling three stitches together, thereby leaving one stitch.

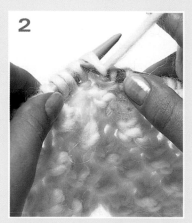

5 Bring the yarn forward to purl and insert the tip of the right needle purlwise, from back to front into all the next three stitches. Purl the three stitches together making one stitch on the right hand needle.

6 These instructions are repeated across the row, to create the raised "popcorns." The same amount of increasings and decreasings are made in the row so that the amount of stitches on the row remains constant. On the next row all the stitches are purled. The increasings and decreasings are worked in the same way but in the opposite order on the next patterned row so that the raised popcorns nestle into each other forming the pattern all over the fabric.

Lace holes

Light and open-lace stitch patterns can be made from yarnover increases combined with an equal number of decreases. When you first try lace knitting, choose a pattern that has reasonably small stitch and row repeats, and includes plain rows of knit or purl as part of the pattern. Yarnover holes can be made in the same way as the buttonhole in Project 2, if worked between two knit stitches. This is called yarn forward (or yf).

Yarnover between two purl stitches

A yarnover can also be made between two purl stitches. This technique is called "yarn round needle" abbreviated as yrn. The result is just like a yarnover made between two knit stitches, but worked on the purl side.

Faggot Lace

Cast on an even number of stitches.
Row 1 K1, *(yf, k2tog), rpt from * to end, k1.
Repeat row 1 for all rows. An effective lacy mesh fabric can be worked using this simple technique of yf combined with a k2tog decrease. As for blackberry popcorn stitch, the first and last stitches of each row are worked without pattern. It is important that you work with an even number of stitches to achieve faggot lace.

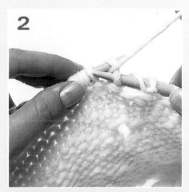

1 After purling a stitch make a yrn by taking the yarn over the top of the right needle to the back of the work then bringing it between the points of the needles to the front again. The yarn should be wrapped around the needle in a counterclockwise direction.

2 The eyelet hole formed beneath the yarn over becomes apparent as you purl the next stitch. The yarnover wrapped around the needle will be worked as a normal stitch on the next row.

CHUNKY KNITS

Poodle Loop Stitch

This loopy knit stitch can impart a shaggy or fluffy pile surface to your knitting; the knitted stitch is not really visible beneath the loops of yarn. The final effect of this technique depends very much on the yarn that you use, as the visible surface is a mass of yarn loops. It is worth experimenting with smooth and textured yarns to achieve different surfaces. The finished loops created with this technique can also be cut to give an alternative shaggy fur effect. This technique can be used for an entire garment but is most often worked as a mock fur trim or used for hats, scarves, and even cuddly knitted toys.

Loop stitch instructions

(Note: When instructions are not given in full, the abbreviation "ml" is sometimes used to mean "make loop.")

The loops are formed on the right side of the work and are therefore usually worked on alternate rows with a plain knit row between. The pictures show the second loop in a row being worked.

1 With the right side facing you, knit into the stitch that is to be worked as a loop, but do not let it slip off the left needle.

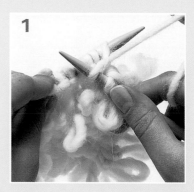

2 Bring the yarn forward between needles and wind once clockwise around your left thumb. Take yarn back again between the needles.

3 Knit again into the same stitch on the left hand needle (making two stitches on the right hand needle).

4 Slip the stitch off the left hand needle to complete a knit stitch and withdraw your thumb from the loop.

5 Place both stitches made on the right hand needle onto the left needle. Do this by inserting the left hand needle into each stitch from left to right and then withdrawing the right needle.

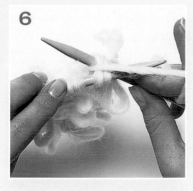

6 Knit both the stitches together by knitting through the back of the stitches. Do this by inserting the right needle into the two stitches, from right to left, keeping the right needle behind the left, and wrapping the yarn as for a knit stitch around the back of the right hand needle.

7 Pull the wrapped yarn through the two stitches as usual, making a new stitch on the right hand needle.

8 Let the worked stitches slip off the left hand needle and the loop stitch is completed. Each stitch can be knitted as a loop in the same way across the row as desired. The next row should be knitted without loops as it is a wrong side row.

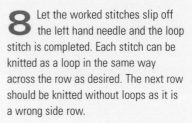

9 To make a cut fringed effect these loops can be snipped with a pair of scissors without danger of the fabric unraveling.

CHUNKY KNITS

Cabling

Cabling is traditionally used in Fisherman knitting, but can be used in many ways to create a range of textural pattern variations. A group of stitches can be crossed over another group in the middle of a row, creating raised stitch patterns. A short double-pointed cable needle is used to transfer the stitches. Once you understand this basic principle of cabling, it is easy to invent and customize cable patterns. These examples show a cable panel four stitches wide in stockinette stitch, worked on a reverse stockinette stitch background. Try working these two simple cables to understand the process of crossing stitches. You will need a double-pointed cable needle the same thickness as your needles.

Cable row, step by step

1 On a right side row, purl to the position of the cable panel—the background is worked in reverse stockinette stitch.

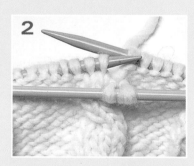

2 Pick up the cable needle and holding it at the front of the work, slip the next two stitches onto it. Do this by inserting the tip of the needle purlwise, from right to left, into the stitches and withdrawing the left hand needle, leaving the cable needle at the front of the work. Take the yarn back, ready to make a knit stitch.

Front cable

This is called "cable 4 front" (abbreviated as c4f) or "cable 4 left" (c4l). The cable crosses from right to left.

Instructions for front cable panel on reverse stockinette stitch ground

Row 1 Right side facing. Purl stitches to position of cable panel, knit 4, purl to end.
Row 2 Wrong side facing. Knit all stitches to position of cable panel, purl 4, knit to end.
Repeat rows as above to desired position of cable row.
Cable row Right side facing. Purl to cable panel, c4f, purl to end.
Next row Wrong side facing. Work as row 2.
Repeat.

3 Knit the next 2 stitches from the left needle.

4 Now knit the two stitches from the cable needle, working the right hand stitch first.

5 The stitches that had been on the cable needle now cross in front of the other stitches on the right hand needle. Continue to work across the rest of the row in purl. You still have the same amount of stitches in the row.

Back cable

This is called "cable 4 back" (abbreviated as c4b) or "cable 4 right" (c4r). The cable crosses from left to right.

Instructions for back cable panel on reverse stockinette stitch ground

Row 1 Right side facing. Purl stitches to position of cable panel, knit 4, purl to end.

Row 2 Wrong side facing. Knit all stitches to position of cable panel, purl 4, knit to end.

Repeat rows as above to desired position of cable row.

Cable row Right side facing. Purl to cable panel, c4b, purl to end.

Next row Wrong side facing. Work as row 2.

Repeat.

1 On a right side row, work to the position of the cable panel.

2 Holding the cable needle at the back of the work, slip the next two stitches onto it. Do this by inserting the tip of the cable needle purlwise, from right to left, into the stitches, and withdraw the left hand needle, leaving the cable needle at the back of the work.

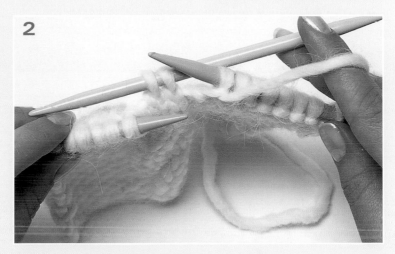

3 Take the yarn back ready to make a knit stitch and knit the next two stitches from the left needle.

4 Now knit the two stitches from the cable needle and put the empty needle aside.

5 The stitches that had been on the cable needle now cross behind the other stitches on the right hand needle. Continue to work across the rest of the row in purl. You still have the same amount of stitches in the row.

PROJECT 6: Blackberry Bomber

This is an easy fitting bomber jacket that's zipped to the collar, and knitted in a chunky blackberry popcorn stitch with contrasting Fisherman (Aran) rib trims. A distinctive fashion statement featuring a scaled-up version of this traditional hand knit stitch. Use a contrast yarn on the ribs for a sporty mood, or capture the spirit of the great outdoors by knitting in a tweedy yarn.

Materials

1175(1310, 1470) yds [1075(1200, 1345) m] chunky wool yarn—color A

Approx 41(44, 48) yds [38(40, 44) m] each in Fisherman yarn—six stripe colors B, C, D, E, F, G = 246(265, 290) yds [225(240, 265) m] total

Needles

1 pair size 7 (4.5 mm) for ribs

1 pair size 11 (8 mm) for main

1 pair size 10 (6 mm) for center front trims

Pins

Tapestry needle

21(22, 23) in. [53(55, 58) cm] open-ended zipper

Strong sewing thread and needle for zipper

Finished measurements

Center front opening 21(22, 23) in. [53(55, 58) cm]

Shoulder seam 2½(3½, 4½) in. [6.5(9, 11.5)cm]

Bust under arm 34(38, 42) in. [86(96, 107) cm]

Sleeve seam 20 in (51 cm) for all sizes

Length to shoulder 25(26, 27) in. [64(66, 68) cm]

Abbreviations

st(s)–stitch(es); **rs**–right side; **k**–knit; **p**–purl; **rpt**–repeat; **rh**–right hand; **k2tog**–knit two stitches together; **p2tog**–purl two stitches together; **p3tog**–purl three stitches together

Gauge

Over blackberry popcorn stitch on size 11 (8 mm) needles and chunky wool yarn: 16 sts and 16 rows to 4 in. (10cm).

Over double rib on size 7 (4.5 mm) needles and Fisherman yarn, 30 sts and 24 rows to 4 in. (10 cm).

Blackberry popcorn stitch

Cast on a multiple of 4 sts + 2sts.

1st row (Rs) P to end.

2nd row K1, *(k1, p1, k1) all in next st, p3tog. Rpt from * to last st, k1.

3rd row P to end.

4th row K1,*p3tog, (k1, p1, k1) all in next st. Rpt from * to last st, k1.

Repeat.

Double rib

Cast on a multiple of 4 + 2 stitches.

Row 1 K2, (p2, k2). Rpt to end.

Row 2 P2, (k2, p2). Rpt to end.

Back

With size 7 (4.5 mm) needles, cast on 70(78, 86) sts in color B (Fisherman yarn).

Rib band

Working in double rib:

Using color B, Fisherman, work 2 rows as follows:

Row 1 K2, (p2, k2) to end.

Row 2 P2 (k2, p2) to end.

Continue in double rib, changing color for striping as follows:

Color C 3 rows.

Color D 3 rows.

Color E 3 rows.

Color F 3 rows.

Color G 2 rows.

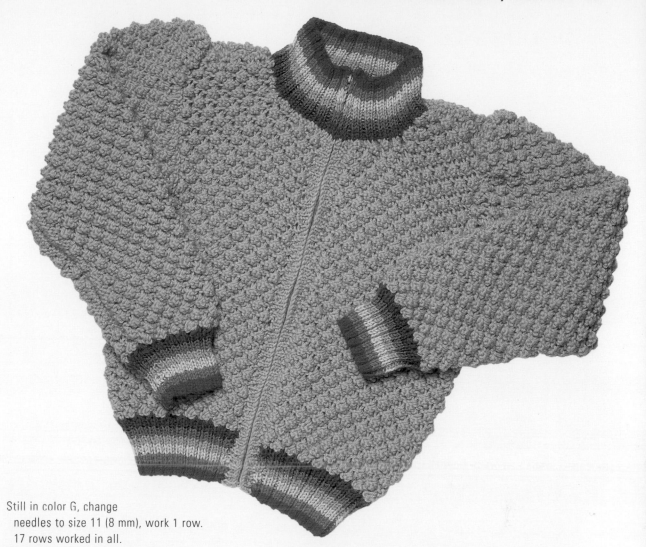

Still in color G, change
   needles to size 11 (8 mm), work 1 row.
   17 rows worked in all.
Change to main yarn A, P 1 row.

Blackberry popcorn stitch pattern
Row 1 (Rs facing) P to end.
Row 2 K1, *(k1, p1, k1) all into next st, p3tog,
   Rpt from * to last st, k1.
Row 3 P to end.
Row 4 K1, *p3tog, (k1, p1, k1) all into next st.
   Rpt from * to last st, k1.
Rpt to row 40.

Armhole shaping
Row 41 Bind off 8 sts, p to end
   = 62(70, 78) sts.
Row 42 K1, **k1, bind off, p3tog, bind off, rpt
   once more from **. 8 sts decreased.
Continue across row, working in blackberry
   popcorn stitch beginning *(k1 p1 k1) all in

next st, p3tog, rpt from * until last st, k1 =
   54(62, 70) sts left at end of row.
Continue working in pattern to row 67(71, 75).

Neck shaping
Right side
Row 68(72, 76) (As row 4) work 13(17, 21) sts
   in pattern (leave these stitches unworked on
   the needle until the left side neck shaping).
Continuing across row, bind off back neck
   as follows:
P3tog, **k1, bind off, p3tog, bind off. Rpt from
   ** six more times. (You will have 1 stitch left
   on the rh needle at end of bind off.)
Continue across row, working into remaining
   stitches for right shoulder as follows:

(K1, p1, k1) into next stitch, *p3tog, (k1, p1, k1) into next st. Rpt from * to last 4 sts, p3tog, k1 = 13(17, 21) sts left on needle.

Row 69(73, 77) P all 13(17, 21) sts.

Row 70(74, 78) *(K1, p1, k1) all in next st, p3tog, rpt from * until last st, k1.

Row 71(75, 79) P all 13(17, 21) sts.

Row 72(76, 80) Bind off all 13(17, 21) sts in pattern as follows ***p3tog, bind off, k1, bind off. Rpt from *** to end.

Left side

Rejoin yarn to unworked stitches on needle.

Row 69(73, 77) P to end.

Row 70(74, 78) K1,*(k1, p1, k1) all in next st, p3tog, rpt from *.

Row 71(75, 79) P to end of row.

Row 72(76, 80) Bind off remaining 13(17, 21) stitches in pattern as follows: K1, ***p3tog, bind off, k1, bind off. Rpt from *** to end.

Front
Left side

With size 7 (4.5 mm) needles and color B Fisherman, cast on 34(38, 42) sts.

Work in double rib, changing color for striping.

Color B 2 rows.

Color C 3 rows.

Color D 3 rows.

Color E 3 rows.

Color F 3 rows.

Color G 2 rows.

Still in color G, change needles to size 11 (8 mm), work 1 row.

Change to main yarn A, p 1 row.

Blackberry popcorn stitch pattern

Row 1 (Rs facing.) P to end.

Row 2 K1, *(k1, p1, k1) all into next st, p3tog. Rpt from * to last st, k1.

Row 3 P to end.

Row 4 K1, *p3tog, (k1, p1, k1) all into next st. Rpt from * to last st, k1.

Rpt to row 40.

Armhole shaping

Row 41 Bind off 8 sts purlwise = 26(30, 34) sts.

Continue working in pattern to row 61.

Neckline shaping

Row 62 K1, **k1, bind off, p3tog, bind off. Rpt once more from **. Continue in pattern as follows: *(k1, p1, k1) all in next st, p3tog. Rpt from * until last st, k1 = 18(22, 26) sts.

Row 63 P to end.

Row 64 K1, p3tog, bind off, k1, bind off, p3tog, bind off *(k1, p1, k1) into next stitch, p3tog. Rpt from * until last st, k1 = 13(17, 21) sts left at end of row.

Row 65 P to end.

Row 66 *(k1, p1, k1) all in next st, p3tog. Rpt from * to last st, k1.

Row 67 P to end.

Row 68 *P3tog, (k1, p1, k1) all in next st. Rpt from * until last stitch, k1.

Row 69 P to end.

Rpt rows 66 to row 69 until row 71(75, 79).

Bind off all stitches in pattern as follows:

Row 72(76, 80) P3tog, *k1, bind off, p3tog, bind off. Rpt from * until last 2 sts, bind off

Right side

Work as left side until row 41.

Armhole shaping

Row 42 K1, **k1, bind off, p3tog, bind off, rpt from ** once more.

Continue across row as follows: *(k1, p1, k1) all in next st, p3tog. Rpt from * until last st, k1 = 26(30, 34) sts.

Continue in pattern until row 62.

Neckline shaping

Row 63 Bind off 8 sts, p to end = 18(22, 26) sts left at end of row.

Row 64 K1, *p3tog, (k1, p1, k1) all in next st, rpt from * until last st, k1.

Row 65 Bind off 5 sts, p to end = 13(17, 21) sts.

Row 66 K1, *(k1, p1, k1) all in next st, p3tog. Rpt from * to end of row.

Row 67 P to end.

Row 68 K1, *p3tog, (k1, p1, k1) all in next st. Rpt from * until end of row.

Row 69 P to end of row.

Rpt last 4 rows until row 71(75, 79).

Row 72(76, 80) Bind off all stitches in pattern as follows: k1, *p3tog, bind off, k1, bind off. Rpt from * to last stitch, bind off.

Sleeves (knit two)

With size 7 (4.5 mm) needles and color B Fisherman, cast on 50(54, 58) sts.

Work in double rib, changing color for striping.

Color B 2 rows.

Color C 3 rows.

Color D 3 rows.

Color E 3 rows.

Color F 3 rows.

Color G 2 rows.

Still in color G, change needles to size 11 (8 mm), work 1 row.

Change to main yarn A, p 1 row.

Blackberry stitch pattern

Row 1 (Rs facing.) P to end.

Row 2 K1, *(k1, p1, k1) all into next st, p3tog. Rpt from * to last st, k1.

Row 3 P to end.

Row 4 K1, *p3tog, (k1, p1, k1) all into next st. Rpt from * to last st, k1.

Increasing

Row 5 Increase 1 stitch at each side as follows: p into front and back of first stitch, p to last stitch, p into front and back of stitch = 52(56, 60) sts.

Row 6 K2, *(k1, p1, k1) all in next st, p3tog. Rpt from * to last 2 sts, k2.

Row 7 P to end of row.

Row 8 K2, *p3tog, (k1, p1, k1) all in next st. Rpt from * to last 2 sts, k2.

Row 9 P to end, increasing 1 st each end of row = 54(58, 62) sts.

Row 10 K3, *(k1, p1, k1) all in next st, p3tog. Rpt from * to last 3 sts, k3.

Row 11 P to end of row.

Row 12 K3, *p3tog, (k1, p1, k1) all in next st.

CHUNKY KNITS

Rpt from * to last 3 sts, k3.

Row 13 P, increasing 1 st each end of row =
56(60, 64) sts.

Row 14 K4, *(k1, p1, k1) all in next st, p3tog.
Rpt from * to last 4 sts, k4.

Row 15 P to end of row.

Row 16 K4 *p3tog, (k1, p1, k1) all in next st.
Rpt from * to last 4 sts, k4.

Row 17 P to end of row increasing 1 st each
end of row = 58(62, 66) sts.

Rpt increasing pattern from row 2 to row 17,
twice more, as established, until row 49 =
74(78, 82) sts.

Rpt increasing pattern from row 2 to row 10
until row 58 = 78(82, 86) sts.

Row 59 P, increasing 1 st each end of row =
80(84, 88) sts.

Row 60 K4, *p3tog, (k1, p1, k1) all in next st,.
rpt from * until last 4 sts, k4.

Row 61 P to end of row increasing 1 st each
end of row = 82(86, 90) sts.

Row 62 K1, *(k1, p1, k1) all in next st, p3tog,
rpt from * until last st, k1.

Row 63 P to end.

Row 64 K1, *p3tog, (k1, p1, k1) all in next st,
rpt from * until last st, k1.

Row 65 P to end.

Rpt rows 62, 63 and 64 until row 68.

Shaping of sleeve head

Row 69 Bind off 20 sts purlwise, p to end.

Row 70 K1, **k1, bind off, p3tog, bind off, rpt
from ** 4 more times, *(k1, p1, k1) all in next
st, p3tog, rpt from * until last st, k1 = 42(46,
50) sts.

Row 71 Bind off 8 sts purlwise, p to end of
row = 34(38, 42) sts.

Row 72 K1, ***p3tog, bind off, k1, bind off,
rpt from *** once more, continue in pattern
*p3tog, (k1, p1, k1) all in next st, rpt from *
until last st, k1 = 26(30, 34) sts.

Row 73 P to end of row.

Row 74 K1, *(k1, p1, k1), p3tog. Rpt from *
until last st, k1.

Row 75 Bind off 4 sts purlwise, p to end =
22(26, 30) sts.

Row 76 K1, p3tog, bind off, knit 1, bind off.
Continue in pattern, *p3tog, (k1, p1, k1) all in
next st, rpt from * until last st, k1 = 18(22,

26) sts.

Row 77 P to end.

Row 78 K1, *(k1, p1, k1) all in next st, p3tog.
Rpt from * to last st, k1.

Row 79 Bind off 4 sts purlwise, p to end =
14(18, 22) sts.

Row 80 K1, p3tog, bind off, knit 1, bind off.
Continue in pattern *p3tog, (k1, p1, k1) all in
next st, rpt from * until last st, k1 = 10(14,
18) sts.

Bind off purlwise.

Assembly and finishing

Block and steam all pieces carefully.

Sew in and trim all ends to neaten.

Center front band

Use size 10 (6 mm) needles and main yarn A.

With right side facing, knit up 72 (74, 76) sts
along straight center front edge of right side
from the bottom of the rib to the neckline as
follows: 12 sts evenly picked off rib, 60(62,
64) sts picked up evenly from main knit. Work
2 rows single rib. Bind off ribwise.

Rpt the same on left side working from top
to bottom, rs facing. Sew in and trim
loose ends.

Join shoulder seams using mattress stitch.

Collar

NOTE At this point it is important to check
that your zipper will fit the center front
opening. Measure the length of the center
front band and subtract this measurement
from the length of the zipper. This is the
depth of rib that you need. The pattern is for
the same depth of rib as the hems. If your
measurement is slightly different, add or
subtract a few rows of striping to achieve
a perfect result.

With color G Fisherman and size 7 (4.5 mm)
needles, knit up 98(106, 114) sts, rs facing
around neck line as follows:

From right center front to right shoulder seam,
knit up 28(32, 36) sts.

Across back neck knit up 42 sts.

From left shoulder seam to left center front,
knit up 28(32, 36) sts.

Work in double rib with Fisherman yarns in
  stripe pattern.
Color G 2 rows.
Color F 3 rows.
Color E 3 rows.
Color D 3 rows.
Color C 3 rows.
Color B 2 rows.
Bind off ribwise in B.
Sew in and trim loose ends.

Sleeves
(See page 71.)
Lay the garment flat. Slot both straight
  ends of sleeve into armhole bound-
  off shaping. Use mattress stitch
  to join, stopping at both
  ends of draw thread.
  Gather sleeve head
  with draw thread to fit
  in armhole. (Measures
  approx 10 ½ in. [27 cm])
Join with mattress
  stitch.

Zipper
(See page 70.)
Position zipper by
  pinning and
  basting.
Stitch into place
  with strong thread,
  using back stitch.

Seams
Join side.

CHUNKY KNITS

Method of Inserting a Zipper

When inserting a zipper, it is important to take your time in order to achieve a professional result. The zipper opening is usually edged with a few stitches or rows of seed, garter, or rib to give a firm edge that does not roll. Choose a zipper that is suitable for your fabric. Color is obviously important but also consider weight. Chunky zippers work really well on chunky knit, but for finer fabrics choose a lighter-weight zipper. Always use a zipper that is the correct length for the opening. Do not stretch the knitting to fit a long zipper; this will not lay flat. Gathering knitting to a short zipper will distort the center front length.

1 With right side facing, lay the knitting onto a flat surface. Pin and baste the edges to meet, using a contrast color sewing thread. Line up the rows or stitch patterns on both sides, and make sure the top and bottom edges are even. Remove pins.

2 Turn work so that the wrong sides are facing you. Lay the right side of the zipper onto the garment. Pin and baste the closed zipper into place, making sure that the zipper teeth lay along the opening. Remove the pins.

3 Turn the work so that the right sides are facing you. Keeping the zipper closed, use a matching, heavy duty sewing thread to backstitch (see page 31) a straight line down the length of the zipper. (A contrast-colored thread has been used her for clarity.)

4 To avoid the thread being visible from the front, pass the stitch on the right side of the work under the ridges of the ribs. When both sides of the zipper are stitched in place, unpick the basting thread.

Making a Button Stand

As an alternative to a zipper, you could try adding a button stand in seed stitch. First, test your gauge with a strip of seed stitch, using one needle size below the main fabric, to check how many stitches you need to pick up down the opening. Before you start knitting, do a test buttonhole to check with your button size and work out where you want to position your buttonholes, spaced evenly along a row.

Making the band with buttonholes

Pick up and knit into the stitches along the opening; work with an odd number of stitches for seed stitch, so all rows are the same.

Working in seed stitch, k1, (p1 k1), repeat to end, for three rows. On the fourth (buttonhole) row, work in seed stitch to the position of the first buttonhole (usually about 3 sts from the edge).

1 Bind off the right number of stitches for your buttonhole, using the usual binding off technique (see page 22). Continue working in seed stitch to the next buttonhole and repeat to the end of the row.

3 Carry on in seed stitch to the next buttonhole and repeat. Continue working buttonholes in this way along row.

4 Work in seed stitch for 3 rows and bind off. To knit a narrower or wider strip, work more or less rows of seed stitch as required.

2 On the next row work in seed stitch to the bound-off stitches and cast on the same number of stitches using a thumb/loop cast-on.

Making the button band

Knit the same number of stitches and rows, without buttonholes, on the other side of the opening. To position buttons accurately, count the stitches between button holes and mark the position with pins, before sewing the buttons into place.

Gathering up knitting

A draw thread is an easy way to gather up knitting before sewing seams. This technique is used on the puffed sleeve head. It is also often used on hats, and when making frills.

Use a strand of smooth yarn or thread in a contrast color, to make a big running stitch around the shaped edge of sleeve head, leaving the ends of thread free to be pulled. The knitting can be eased along the thread and gathered to the correct length. Remove the draw thread once the seam is sewn to position.

CHUNKY KNITS

PROJECT 7: Afghan Coat

An extravagant use of loopy poodle knit stitch trims the front opening and cuffs of this striking coat. Vertical lines of double rib and a long-line, edge-to-edge opening create a leaner silhouette. Position the belt and belt loops to tie low on the hip or fasten with corded ties.

Materials
Main yarn
1100(1245, 1300) yds [1000(1140, 1190) m]
  chunky wool yarn
1 pair size 10½ (7 mm) needles

Trim
165(219, 275) yds [150 (198, 250) m] extra
  chunky wool fleece yarn
1 pair size 10½ (7.5 mm) needles
Tapestry needle

Finished measurements
Center back length 38(39, 40) in.
  [96(99, 101.5) cm]
Bust/hip 39½(43½, 48½) in.
  [(100, 110.5, 123) cm]
Sleeve seam 19 in. (48 cm) all sizes

Gauge
Main yarn
Over double rib on size 10½ (7 mm) needles,
  when blocked to size: 14 sts and 16 rows to
  4 in. (10 cm)

Trim
Over loopy stitch (see page 60) on size 10½ (7.5
  mm): 8 sts and 12 rows to 4 in. (10 cm).

Abbreviations
st(s)–stitch(es); **k**–knit; **p**–purl; **sl1, k1, psso**–slip 1, knit 1, pass slip stitch over; **k2tog**–knit 2 stitches together; **p2tog**–purl 2 stitches together; **ws**–wrong side; **rs**–right side; **rpt**–repeat; **beg**–beginning

Loopy knit technique (cast on loosely)
Loops form on the right side of work.
Row 1 Knit.
Row 2 Loop row:
Knit stitch but do not let loop drop off left

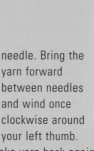

needle. Bring the yarn forward between needles and wind once clockwise around your left thumb. Take yarn back again between needles and knit again into the same stitch on the left hand needle, (making two stitches from the original one). Slip stitch off the left hand needle. Place both stitches back on the left needle and knit both together through the back of the two stitches. Repeat across row.

Back
Cast on 70(78, 86) stitches in main yarn.
Work in double rib.
Row 1 P2, *(k2, p2), rpt from * to end.
Row 2 K2, *(p2, k2), rpt from * to end.
Repeat rows 1 and 2 to row 110.
Length can be adjusted here if desired.

Armhole shaping
Row 111 Bind off 2 sts at beg of row (1 st on
  right hand needle), k1, *(p2, k2), rpt from * to
  last 2 sts, p2.
Row 112 Bind off 2 sts at beg of row (1 st on
  right hand needle), p1, *(k2, p2), rpt from *
  to end.
Row 113 K2, sl1, p1, psso, k2, *(p2, k2), rpt
  from * to end.
Row 114 P2, sl1, k1, psso, p2, *(k2, p2), rpt
  from * to last 3 sts, k1, p2.
Row 115 K2, sl1, k1, psso, k1, *(p2, k2), rpt
  from * to last 3 sts, p1, k2.
Row 116 P2, sl1, p1, psso, p1, *(k2, p2), rpt
  from * to last 2 sts, p2.
Row 117 K2, sl1, k1, psso, p2, *(k2, p2), rpt
  from * to last 4 sts, k4.
Row 118 P2, sl1, p1, psso, k2, *(p2, k2), rpt

from * to last 3 sts, p3.

Row 119 K2, sl1, p1, psso, p1, *(k2, p2), rpt from * to last 3 sts, k3.

Row 120 P2, sl1, k1, psso, k1, p2, *(k2, p2), rpt from * to end.

You should have 58(66, 74) sts.

Continue working in rib to row 154 (158, 162).
Bind off all stitches ribwise.

Front

Left side

Cast on 28(32, 36) sts and work in double rib.

Row 1 *(P2, k2), rpt from * to end.

Continue double rib as established to row 106.

Adjust length here to match back, if desired.

Row 107 *(P2, k2), rpt from * to end.

Row 108 P2tog, k2 (p2, k2) to end = 27(31, 35) sts.

Work 2 rows in double rib as established without shaping.

Armhole shaping

Row 111 Bind off 2 sts at beginning of row (1 st on right hand needle), k1, *(p2, k2), rpt from * to last 3 sts, p2, k1 = 25(29, 33) sts.

Row 112 P1, *(k2, p2), rpt from * to end.

Row 113 K2, sl1, p1, psso, (k2, p2) to last stitch, k1 = 24(28, 32) sts.

Row 114 K2tog, k1, p2, *(k2, p2), rpt from * to last 3 sts, k1, p2 = 23(27, 31) sts.

Row 115 K2, sl1, k1, psso, k1, *(p2, k2), rpt from * to last 2 sts, p2 = 22(26, 30) sts.

Row 116 *(K2, p2), rpt from * to last 2 sts, p2.

Row 117 K2, sl1, k1, psso, p2, *(k2, p2), rpt from * to end = 21(25, 29) sts.

Row 118 *(K2, p2), rpt from * to last st, p1.

Row 119 K2, sl1, p1, psso, p1, *(k2, p2), rpt from * to end = 20(24, 28) sts.

Row 120 K2tog, p2, *(k2, p2), rpt from * to end = 19(23, 27) sts.

Row 121 *(K2, p2), rpt from * to last 3 sts, k2, p1.

Row 122 K1, p2, *(k2, p2), rpt from * to end.

Row 123 *(K2, p2) , rpt from * to last 3 sts, k2, p1.

Row 124 P2tog, p1, *(k2, p2), rpt from * to end = 18(22, 26) sts.

Row 125 *(K2, p2) , rpt from * to last 2 sts, k2.

Continue working in double rib to row 154(158, 162).

Shoulder shaping
Row 155(159, 163) Bind off 6(8, 8) sts ribwise at beg row, rib to end of row = 12(14, 18) sts.
Row 156(160, 164) P2, *(k2, p2) rpt from * to end.
Row 157(161, 162) Bind off 6(7, 9) sts ribwise at beg of row, rib to end of row = 6(7, 9) sts.
Bind off remaining 6(7, 9) sts ribwise.

Right side
Work as for left, reversing shapings.

Sleeves (knit two)
Loopy cuff
Cast on 21(23, 25) sts with fleece yarn on size 10½ (7.5 mm) needles.
Row 1 Knit.
Row 2 Make loops in all stitches.
Repeat rows 1 and 2 until you have knitted 8 rows.

Main yarn
Change yarn to main color and size 10½ (7 mm) needles.
Row 1 Increase by working twice into each stitch as follows:
Purl into back and front of first st, knit into back and front of second stitch. Work across row in this way = 42(46, 50) sts.
Row 2 P2, *(k2, p2) rpt from * to end.
Row 3 K2, *(p2, k2) rpt from * to end.
Row 4 Keeping in double rib, increase 1 st at both ends of row = 44(48, 52) sts.
Keeping rib pattern correct, increase 1 st at both ends of every 4th row, until you have 64 rows = 74(78, 82) sts.
Work 2 rows in double rib, finishing with a wrong side row.
Adjust sleeve length here if desired.
Rows 67–74 Working in rib, decrease 1 st at beg and 1 st at end of each row for these 8 rows, leaving 58(62, 66) sts.
Bind off ribwise.

Front trim and collar
Right
Cast on 5(7, 7) sts on size 10½ (7.5 mm) needles in trim yarn.

Row 1 Knit.
Row 2 Make loops in all stitches. Adjust length here if you have adjusted length of the coat.
Row 67(71, 75) Ws facing, increase 1st at beg of row, knit row.
Work 9 rows in pattern.
Row 77(81, 85) Ws facing, increase 1 st at beg of row.
Work 9 rows in pattern.
Row 87(91, 95) Ws facing, increase 1 st at beginning of row.
Continue to row 110(114, 118), or until band matches length of front piece.
Work 10(12, 14) more rows in pattern, or until band reaches centre back of neck. Bind off.

Left
As right side to row 66.
Rows 67(71, 75), 77(81, 85), 87(91, 95) increase 1 st at end of row.
Complete to match right side.

Assembly
Block and steam pieces gently on wrong side to give a flatter fabric.
Join shoulder seams using mattress stitch.
Join front trim pieces at back neck using mattress stitch.
Join trim to fronts and back neck, matching center back seam to center of back neck.
Using mattress stitch and making sure that center of sleeves meet the shoulder seam, sew sleeves into armholes. Make sure that first two rows of decreasing on sleeves meet bound-off stitches of armholes.
Join side and sleeve seams. Steam all seams lightly.

Fastenings
You can choose between a belt and belt loops or corded ties to fasten the coat as desired.

Belt
Single rib, 1½ in. (4 cm) wide and 57(61, 65) in. [145(155, 165) cm] long.
Cast on 9 sts.
Row 1 K1, *(p1, k1), rpt from *to end.
Row 2 P1, *(k1, p1) , rpt from *to end.

Repeat until the belt measures 57(61, 65) in.
  [145(155, 165) cm].
Bind off.

Belt loops (make two)
(See page 76.)
Take 20 in. (50 cm) of main yarn, fold double
  and twist to make an 8 in. (20 cm) length of
  cord. Thread ends through side seam in two
  places at low waist point, to fit width of
  belt, and knot ends together on wrong side.
  Trim ends.

Corded ties (make six alike)
Take 71 in. (180 cm) of main yarn, fold into
  four, and twist and knot to make a 10 in. (25
  cm) length of cord.
Attach first cord to right
  side center front
  trim, level with
  underarm seam.
Attach second cord to
  left side to match.
Attach remaining cords in
  two pairs at 6 in. (15 cm)
  intervals down center front.

Making Corded Ties and Belt Loops

The Afghan Coat can be fastened with a belt or with corded ties, or both! The twisted cord can be used for both trims. It is a useful technique for making ties from the same yarn as your garment or from a contrasting one. You can experiment with making cords of different thicknesses, and using different yarn types and colors to suit the garment that you are making. This type of cord can also be used for drawstrings on knitwear and accessories and, worked on a bigger scale, it can even be used to make a tie belt. Ties and cords can also be made by braiding yarns together, exactly like braiding hair.

Twisted cord

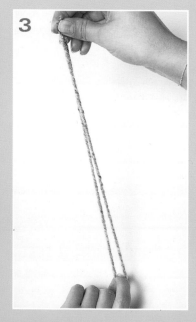

1 Cut or fold the required number of strands. Allow about two and a half times the desired length of the cord. Knot or fold the strands at both ends and fix one end to a firm surface using masking tape, or tie to an available hook or door handle.

2 Take hold of the free end and twist until tight.

3 Holding the twisted cord exactly in the center with one hand, bring both knotted ends to meet.

4 The two halves will twist together to make the cord. Smooth out evenly and tie the loose ends together.

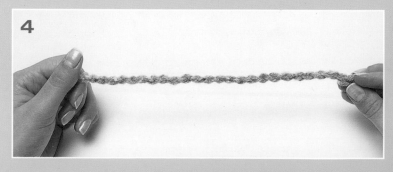

To attach the belt loops

Make two 8 in. (20 cm) lengths of cord.

1 On the side seam, mark above and below the desired position of the belt, using two pins 3 in. (8 cm) apart. Using fingers or a crochet hook, thread ends through the stitches of the side seam from right side to wrong side, as marked.

2 Knot the ends firmly together on wrong side. Trim neatly to finish.

To attach corded ties

For the Afghan Coat, make six long ties as instructed, trimming to leave a neat tassel at the knotted end of each cord.

Note that these ties are made thicker than the belt loops, using more strands of yarn. You can vary the amount of strands twisted together to achieve different weights of ties.

Mark the desired position of ties on front trim, two stitches in from the center front edge, using pins. Make sure that the left and right ties are positioned accurately.

2 Push the tasseled end of the cord through the loop at the folded end.

1 Working from the right side and using a crochet hook or fingers, thread the tip of the folded end of cord through the marked stitch to the wrong side and back through to the right side through the stitch above.

3 Pull the cord right through to tighten and fix into position.

CHUNKY KNITS

PROJECT 8: Kids' Poncho

This is a flower-scattered poncho that will suit girls of all ages. Easily knitted in moss stitch, the decorative flower motifs and leafy stem ties are all applied after the knitting has been completed. The techniques introduced offer simple ways to experiment with seemingly complex patterning.

Materials

960 yards (880 m) chunky wool yarn
1 pair size 11 (8 mm) needles
1 pair size 10½ (7 mm) needles for rib and flowers

Gauge

Over moss stitch on size 11 (8 mm) needles: 14 sts and 18 rows to 4 in. (10 cm)

Moss stitch

Row 1 (P1, k1), rpt to end of row.
Row 2 (P1, k1), rpt to end of row.
Row 3 (K1, p1), rpt to end of row.
Row 4 (K1, p1), rpt to end of row.

Finished size

(To fit ages 4–6.)
Center front neck to wrist measurement
16 ½ in. (42 cm)

Abbreviations

k–knit; **p**–purl; **st(s)**–stitch(es); **rpt**–repeat;
psso–pass slip stitch over; **yf**–yarn forward;
k2tog–knit 2 stitches together; **p2tog**–purl 2
stitches together; **sl1, k1, psso**–slip 1, knit 1,
pass slip stitch over

Poncho

Poncho knitted in four identical quarters as follows:

Cast on 89 sts on size 11 (8 mm) needles.
Row 1 P1, (k1, p1) rpt to end (end on p).
Row 2 K2tog, (p1, k1) to last 2 sts. K2 tog.
Rpt rows 1 and 2 up to row 40, decreasing both ends of alternate rows, ending with k2tog row and leaving 49 sts on needle.
Row 41 K2tog, (p1, k1) to last 2 sts, k2tog.
Row 42 P2tog, (k1, p1) to last 2 sts, p2tog.
Row 43 P2tog (k1, p1) to last 2 sts, p2tog.
Row 44 K2tog (p1, k1), to last 2 sts, k2tog.

Rpt rows 41–44 three more times (to row 56).
Row 57 Rpt row 41 (leaving 15 sts).

Neck

Change to size 10½ (7 mm) needles and work single rib as follows:
Row 58 K1, (p1, k1) to end of row.
Row 59 P1, (k1, p1) to end of row.
Rpt rows 58 and 59 for total 6 rows rib.
Bind off ribwise.

Flowers

Make 26 petals and 4 centers. (Six petals will be used on ties.)
Use size 10½ (7 mm) needles and same yarn.

Petals

Cast on 3 sts.
Row 1 K all sts.
Row 2 P all sts.
Row 3 K1, yf, k1, yf, k1.
Row 4 P.
Row 5 K2, yf, k1, yf, k2.
Row 6 P.
Row 7 K3, yf, k1, yf, k3.
Row 8 P.
Row 9 K4, yf, k1, yf, k4 = 11 sts.
Row 10 P.
Row 11 K.
Row 12 P.
Row 13 K3, sl1, k1, psso, k1, k2tog, k3.
Row 14 P.
Row 15 K2, sl1, k1, psso, k1, k2tog, k2.
Row 16 P.
Row 17 K1, sl1, k1, psso, k1, k2tog, k1.
Row 18 P.
Row 19 Sl1, k1, psso, k1, k2tog.
Row 20 P3.

Row 21 Sl1, k2tog, psso. Bind off (break yarn, pull end of yarn through stitch).

Centers

Cast on 3 sts.

Row 1 K into front and back of every st = 6 sts.

Row 2 K into front and back of every st = 12 sts.

Row 3 Sl first stitch, k to last st, sl last st.

Row 4 K2tog along row = 6 sts.

Row 5 K2tog along row = 3 sts.

Row 6 Sl1, k2tog, psso.

Fasten off.

Finishing and assembly

Block and steam all pieces to equal size.

Join 3 seams from bottom edge to top of rib, using mattress stitch, working one stitch from the edge.

Join 4th (center front) seam from bottom edge to 2½ in. (6 cm) below rib for neck opening.

Using five petals for each flower, arrange one flower on each of the four panels, as in diagram. Stitch into place with yarn. Add one center in the middle of each flower, just covering the tips of the petals.

Note: The six spare petals will be used for the leafy ties.

Leafy ties

(See page 80.)

Make two lengths of braid 8 in. (20 cm) long. Knot at ends.

Take the six spare petal shapes to make leaf detail.

Put two petals together to make a double-sided leaf. Starting at the base of the leaf, overstitch around edge, and leave a tiny opening. Push the knot of the braid into the opening and stitch into place. Repeat with two other petal shapes to make the other braid stem.

Stitch third leaf in place ¾ in. (2 cm) along from leaf on one braid.

Thread tips of other ends of braids through edge of rib opening from right to wrong side of rib neck, and stitch knotted ends in place on wrong side.

CHUNKY KNITS

Making Leafy Ties

Ties are a convenient and simple way to fasten knitwear. The decorative ties for the kid's poncho are trimmed with knitted petal shapes and braided yarn. They are attached to either side of the neck opening at the center front. For an adult's garment, longer ties can be threaded through the knitting all around a neckline, but for safety this method should not be used for a child.

Take six 10 in. (25 cm) lengths of yarn, knot at one end, and braid together for 8 in. (20 cm). Knot at end and trim. Block, steam, and sew in ends of the petal shapes before assembling

1 Put two petals together to make a double-sided leaf. Starting at the base of the leaf, overstitch right around edge, and leave a tiny opening at the base.

2 Push a knotted end of braid into the opening and stitch securely in place, closing the opening. Repeat to make another braided stem.

3 Overstitch remaining two petal shapes all around to make another leaf and stitch into place ¾ in. (2 cm) along from end leaf on one braid.

4 Thread tips of other ends of braids through edge of rib neck opening from right to wrong side.

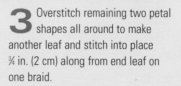

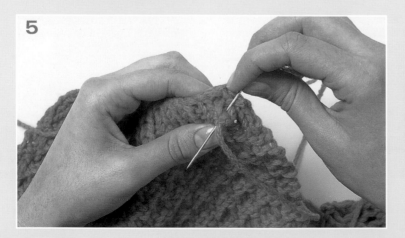

5 Stitch the knotted ends into place on the wrong side and sew in all loose ends.

Applying Flowers

These shaped stockinette stitch flowers are an easy way of adding surface decoration to knitted items. They work best applied onto a textured surface or reverse stockinette stitch surfaces. You could try working them in contrast color or following the alternative petal pattern for a variation.

Block, steam, and sew in ends of all petals and fabric before stitching to place. Pin petal to position onto right side of fabric.

1 Thread a tapestry needle with yarn and bring through from the wrong side of main fabric, up through the center of an edge stitch of the petal. Catch into a stitch on the main fabric and up through the next edge stitch of the petal. Continue in this way around the petal and take end through to wrong side of fabric to secure.

2 Stitch the center pompom into place and secure ends on wrong side.

Ringing the Changes

The poncho pattern can also be worked in reverse stockinette stitch with a moss stitch border. You can have fun varying the positions of the flowers. Also, try working this alternative petal shape, with increasing worked by knitting into the stitch below as "m1" (see page 25), rather than a yarn over.

Alternative petals
Cast on 2 stitches.
Row 1 K1, yf, k1.
Row 2 P.
Row 3 K1, m1, k1, m1, k1.
Row 4 P.
Row 5 K2, m1, k1, m1, k2.
Row 6 P.
Row 7 K3, m1, k1, m1, k3 = 9 sts.
Row 8 P.
Row 9 K.
Row 10 P.
Row 11 K.
Row 12 P.
Row 13 K3, sl1, k2tog, psso, k3 = 7 sts.
Row 14 P.
Row 15 K2, sl1, k2tog, psso, k2 = 5 sts.
Row 16 P.

Row 17 K1, sl1, k2tog, psso, k1.
Row 18 P.
Row 19 Sl1, k2tog, psso.
Bind off.

Stitch these petals in the same way, with a center pompom, but try using four for each flower.

PROJECT 9: Lacy Cowl Neck Sweater

Soft and light, this fluffy mohair is knitted in a loose knit lace pattern with giant draped cowl neck, and deep ribbed hem and cuffs. You can enhance this frothy, feminine sweater by gently brushing the mohair surface to create ultimate luxury, or use striping to accent the wavy lines in the stitch structure.

Materials
660(865) yds [600(790) m] chunky luxury mohair yarn
1 pair size 8 (5 mm) needles for collar
1 pair size 9 (5.5 mm) needles
1 pair size 10½ (7 mm) needles
Two stitch holders (for neck)
Tapestry needle

Gauge
Over lacy pattern on size 10½ (7 mm) needles: 12¾ sts and 20 rows to 4 in. (10 cm)

Lacy pattern
Cast on a multiple of 12 sts + 1 st.
Row 1 K.
Row 2 P.
Row 3 Lace stitch pattern: K1, (k2tog, k2tog, yf, k1, yf, k1, yf, k1, yf, k2tog, k2tog, k1).
Row 4 K.
Rpt rows 1–4.

Finished measurements
Length at center back 20½(22) in. [52(56 cm)]
Chest at underarm 37½(45) in. [95(114) cm]
Sleeve seam 20½ in. (52 cm)

Abbreviations
st(s)–stitch(es); **rs**–right side; **ws**–wrong side;
k–knit; **p**–purl; **rpt**–repeat; **k2tog**–knit two stitches together; **p2tog**–purl two stitches together; **yf**–bring yarn forward to make a yarn over; **rpt**—repeat

Back
Single rib
Using size 9 (5.5 mm) needles, cast on 61(73) sts.
Row 1 K1, (p1, k1) to end.
Row 2 P1, (k1, p1) to end.
Work 20 rows rib as established.

Start lacy pattern
Using size 10½ (7 mm) needles:
Row 1 K.
Row 2 P.
Row 3 K1, (k2tog, k2 tog, yf, k1, yf, k1, yf, k1, yf, k2tog, k2tog, k1) to end.
Row 4 K.
Rpt rows 1–4 to row 68 (or until work measures 18 in. (46 cm), ending on row 4 of established pattern).
Rpt rows 1–4 for 12 (24) more rows, to row 80(94).

Shape shoulder
Decrease 6 sts at beginning of next 4 rows then 6(9) sts at beginning of following 2 rows keeping in pattern as follows:
Row 81(95) Bind off 6(6) sts, k to end.
Row 82(96) Bind off 6(6) sts purlwise, p to end.
Row 83(97) Bind off 6(6) sts, continue working in row 3 of pattern: k1, (k2tog, k2tog, yf, k1, yf, k1, yf, k1, yf, k2tog, k2tog, k1) to last 6 sts, k last 6 sts.
Row 84(98) Bind off 6(6) sts, k to end.
Row 85(99) Bind off 6(9) sts knitwise, k to end.
Row 86(100) Bind off 6(9) sts purlwise, put remaining 25(31) sts on holder for back neck.

Front
As Back to row 68 (or until work measures 18 in. (46 cm), ending on row 4 of established pattern).
Work next 16 rows as follows:
Row 69 Work in pattern (knit) for first 23(26)sts.
Put remaining 38(47) sts on holder and turn work.

Left side neck shaping

Row 70 P2tog, p to end = 22(25) sts.

First size only **Row 71** K1, (k2tog, k2tog yf, k1, yf, k1, yf, k1, yf, k2tog, k2tog, k1), k2 tog, k2tog, yf, k1, yf, k2, k2tog = 21 sts.

Second size only **Row 71** K1, (k2tog, k2tog yf, k1, yf, k1, yf, k1, yf, k2tog, k2tog, k1), k2tog, k2tog, yf, k1, yf, k1,yf, k2, k2tog, k2tog = 24 sts.

Row 72 K2tog, k to end = 20(23) sts.

Row 73 K to last 2 sts, k2tog = 19(22) sts.

Row 74 P2tog, p to end = 18(21)sts.

First size only **Row 75** K1, (k2tog, k2tog, yf, k1, yf, k1, yf, k1, yf, k2tog, k2tog, k1), k2tog, yf, k3 = 18 sts.

Second size only **Row 75** K1, (k2tog, k2tog yf, k1, yf, k1, yf, k1, yf, k2tog, k2tog, k1), k2tog, k2tog, yf, k1, yf, k3 = 21 sts.

Row 76 K.

Row 77 K.

Row 78 P.

First size only **Row 79** K1, (k2 tog, k2 tog, yf, k1, yf, k1, yf, k1, yf, k2tog, k2tog, k1), k2tog, yf, k3.

Second size only **Row 79** K1, (k2tog, k2tog yf, k1, yf, k1, yf, k1, yf, k2tog, k2tog, k1), k2tog, yf, k1, yf, k3

Row 80 K.

Second size only Repeat rows 77–80 three more times (to row 92).

Row 81(93) Bind off 6 sts, k to end = 12(15) sts.

Row 82(94) P.

Row 83(95) Bind off 6 sts (one st on rh needles), k2tog, yf, k3 = 6(9) sts.

Row 84(96) K.

Bind off remaining 6(9) sts.

Right side neck shaping

Put center 15(21) sts on holder for neck.

Row 69 K to end.

Row 70 P to last 2 sts, p2 tog = 22(25) sts.

First size only **Row 71** K2 tog, k2, yf, k1, yf, k2tog, k2tog, k1, (k2tog, k2tog, yf, k1, yf, k1, yf, k1, yf, k2tog, k2tog, k1) = 20 sts.

Second size only **Row 71** K2tog, k2tog, k2, yf, k1, yf, k1, yf, k2tog, k2tog, k1, (k2tog, k2tog yf, k1, yf, k1, yf, k1, yf, k2tog, k2tog, k1)= 24 sts.

Row 72 K to last 2 sts, k2tog = 19(23) sts.

Row 73 K2tog, k to end.

Row 74 P to last 2 sts, p2tog = 18(22) sts.

First size only **Row 75** K3, yf, k2tog, k1, (k2tog, k2tog, yf, k1, yf, k1, yf, k1, yf, k2tog, k2tog, k1) = 18 sts.

Second size only **Row 75** K3, yf, k1, yf, k2tog, k2tog, k1, (k2tog, k2tog yf, k1, yf, k1, yf, k1, yf, k2tog, k2tog, k1= 21 sts.

Row 76 K.

Row 77 K.

Row 78 P.

First size only **Row 79** K3, yf, k2tog, k1, (k2tog, k2tog, yf, k1, yf, k1, yf, k1, yf, k2tog, k2tog, k1).

Second size only **Row 79** K3, yf, k1, yf, k2tog, k2tog, k1, (k2tog, k2tog yf, k1, yf, k1, yf, k1, yf, k2tog, k2tog, k1.

Row 80 K.

Row 81 K.

Second size only Repeat rows 77–80 3 more times (to row 93).

Row 82(94) Bind off 6 sts purlwise, p to end = 12(15) sts.

First size only **Row 83** K3, yf, k2tog, k1, k2tog, k2tog, yf, k1, yf, k1.

Second size only **Row 95** K3, yf, k2tog, k1, k2tog, k2tog, yf, k1, yf, k1, yf, k1, k2tog.

Row 84(96) Bind off 6(6) (one st on rh needle) sts, k5 = 6(9) sts.

Bind off remaining 6(9) sts.

Sleeves (knit two)

On size 9 (5.5 mm) needles, cast on 37(49) sts working in single rib as follows:

Row 1 P1, (k1, p1) to end.

Row 2 K1, (p1, k1) to end.

Rpt rows 1 and 2 to row 16.

Begin pattern using size 10½ (7 mm) needles.

Row 1 K all stitches.

Row 2 P all stitches.

Row 3 K1, (*k2tog, k2 tog, yf, k1, yf, k1, yf, k1, yf, k2tog, k2tog, k1*) to end.

Row 4 K.

Row 5 Increase 1 st at beginning of row by knitting twice into st. K to last st, increase 1 st at end of row by knitting twice into last st = 39(51) stitches.

Row 6 P.

Row 7 K2, rpt pattern from * to * to last stitch, k1.

Row 8 K.

Row 9 K.

Row 10 P.

Row 11 Rpt row 7.

Row 12 K.

Row 13 Rpt row 5, increasing at beginning and end of row = 41(53) stitches.

Row 14 P.

Row 15 K3, rpt pattern from * to * to last 2 sts, k2.

Row 16 K.

Continue in pattern as established, work all increased stitches in knit stitch on lace pattern rows, as follows:

Row 19 K3, rpt pattern from * to *, k2.

Row 21 Increase at both ends of row = 43(55) sts.

Row 23 K4, rpt pattern from * to *, k3.

Row 27 K4, rpt pattern from * to *, k3.

Row 29 Increase at both ends of row = 45(57) sts.

Row 31 K5, rpt pattern from * to *, k4.

Row 35 K5, rpt pattern from * to *, k4.

Row 37 Increase at both ends of row = 47(59) sts.

Row 39 K6, rpt pattern from * to *, k5.

Row 43 K6, rpt pattern from * to *, k5.

Row 45 Increase at both ends of row = 49(61) sts.

Row 47 K7, rpt pattern from * to *, k6.

Row 51 K7, rpt pattern from * to *, k6.

Row 53 Increase at both ends of row = 51(63) sts.

Row 55 K8, rpt pattern from * to *, k7.

Row 59 K8, rpt pattern from * to *, k7.

Row 61 Increase at both ends of row = 53(65) sts.

Row 63 K9, rpt pattern from * to *, k8.

Row 64 K.

Row 65 K.

Row 66 P.

Row 67 K9, rpt pattern from * to *, k8.

Row 68 K.

Continue in pattern (rpt rows 65–68) with no shaping to row 84(92) (or until work measures 20½(22) in. [52(56) cm] or required length, ending with a knit row).

Bind off loosely.

Finishing and assembly

Block pieces and steam gently to shape.

Collar

Join right shoulder seam using mattress stitch.
Using size 8 (5 mm) needles and with rs of
work facing, begin at left shoulder.
Knit up 18(25) sts evenly down left front neck.
Knit across 15(21) sts from stitch holder
   at front.
Knit up 18(25) sts evenly up right front neck.
Knit across 25(31) sts from holder for
   back neck.
There should now be 76(102) sts on the
   needle.

Work in single rib

Row 1 (K1, p1) to end.
Continue in single rib for 8 more rows
   to row 9.

Increasing for cowl front

Row 10 P1, k2, p3, *(k twice into stitch,
   p1, p twice into stitch, p1)*, rpt
   between *and* 9(14) more times
   (increasing 20(30) sts).
For first size only (K2, p3) to
   end. You now have
   96 sts.
For second size only (k2,
   p3) to last st, k1.
   You now have 132 sts.
For first size only **Row 11**
   (K3, p2) to last stitch,
   k1.
For second size only **Row 11**
   P1, (k3, p2) to last st, k1,
For first size only **Row 12** P1, (k2,
   p3) to end.
For second size only **Row 12** P1, (k2, p3)
   to last st, k1.
Change to size 10½ (7 mm) needles.
Work in rib as rows 11 and 12 for 30 more
   rows to row 42. Bind off loosely, ribwise.

Assembly using mattress stitch

Join left shoulder and collar seam, sew collar
   seam from ws as it will fold over.
Matching center point of sleeve with shoulder
   seam, attach sleeves to body.
Join side and sleeve seams.
Sew in loose ends
   to finish.

Adapting the Design

The lace pattern for this garment can be transformed by striping color in different proportions, enhancing the wavy row structure. This is an opportunity to experiment with a range of colors in mohair.

Wide Stripe

Work rows 1–4 of the lace pattern as in first color, then work next four rows in contrast color. Repeat to achieve a bold, wavy stripe effect.

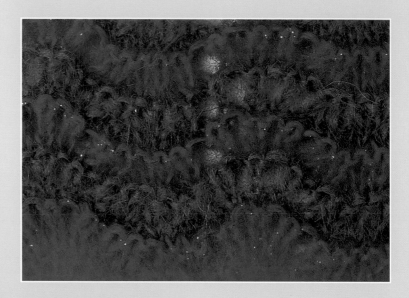

Brushing Mohair

Mohair can be made even more fluffy by brushing with a mohair brush. Some mohair yarns are supplied waxed to reduce shedding while you knit, these should be washed before brushing and wearing. Work carefully, brushing down the fabric, from top to bottom, and holding the fabric flat with your other hand.

Fine Stripe

Work first three rows of lace pattern in main color, then work fourth (knit) row in contrast color to give a fine single stripe. This example has been brushed to give a more subtle color mix.

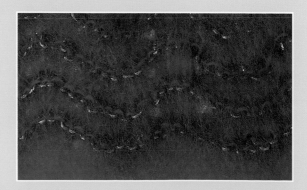

Working Lace Holes on a Rib

Lace holes can be worked into a rib trim or garment without distoring the finished measurements. It is very easy to put the lace holes into this k3, p2 rib as the yarnover is always worked as a "yf" between two knit stitches in the same way as the eyelet buttonhole in Project 2.

The rib cowl can be knitted with yarnover holes, to add more lace detail.

When you reach row 11 of the cowl and alternate odd numbered rows of the 2x3 rib, replace (k3, p2) with (k1, yf, k2tog), making a yarnover hole in the middle of the three knit stitches.

Row 12 and all even numbered rows of the rib are worked as usual (k2, p3).
Row 13 and alternate odd numbered rows are worked as usual (k3, p2).

Lace Patterns as Charts

The instructions for the lace pattern can be written into the pattern using abbreviations, however a chart is often used instead. Each square of the chart represents a stitch and each row represents a row of stitches. A chart is numbered up the side to represent row numbers, and is read by starting at the bottom and working to the top, just as knitting grows. The rows numbered on the right hand side represent right side rows and are read from right to left. The rows that are numbered on the left represent wrong side rows and are read from left to right. The shaded area shows edge stitches that are needed to balance the pattern. The unshaded areas show the multiple of stitches that form the repeat. This multiple is written beneath the chart; in this example the multiple is 12 plus one, so the 12 unshaded stitches are repeated across the row and the one shaded stitch is used to balance the repeat at the edge. A key to the chart is usually given with a pattern.

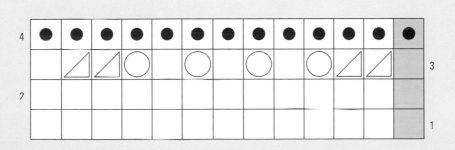

Knit on rs row
Purl on ws row

Purl on rs row
Knit on ws row

Knit two stitches together

Yarnover or "yf"

CHUNKY KNITS

PROJECT 10: Cable V-neck

Fashion's interpretation of a traditional English cricket sweater, this fitted sweater with a deep V-neck looks good worn on its own or over a shirt. The giant cable has a twisted rope-like appearance easily achieved using the basic front cable explained in Textural Stitch Techniques. Use a cream color wool for an updated cricket style. Try adding striped ribs for a sporty look or work in a rich color yarn for a more sophisticated version.

Materials
652(766, 901) yds [595(700, 825)m] extra
   chunky wool mix yarn
1 pair size 10½ (7 mm) needles
1 pair size 11 (8 mm) needles
Tapestry needle
1 x stitch holder
1 x size 11 (8 mm) cable needle

Gauge
Over stockinette stitch on size 11 (8 mm) needles:
   12 sts and 16 rows to 4 in. (10 cm)

Finished measurements
Back length 23½(24½, 25½) in. [59(62, 65) cm]
Sleeve seam 19(20, 21) in. [48(50, 53) cm]
Bust at underarm 34(38, 42) in. [86(96, 107) cm]

Abbreviations
st(s)–stitch(es); **k**–knit; **p**–purl; **rpt**–repeat;
st.st–stockinette stitch; **dec**–decrease;
inc–increase; **k2tog**–knit 2 stitches together;
p2tog–purl 2 stitches together; **rs**–right side;
ws–wrong side; **sl**–slip; **patt**–pattern

Back
Cast on 56(62, 68) sts using size 10½ (7 mm)
   needles.
Work first row as follows. This will be the wrong
   side of work.

Rib
Row 1 (k2, p4) rpt to last 2 sts, k2.
Row 2 (p2, k4) rpt to last 2 sts, p2.
These 2 rows form rib. Rpt 3 more times = 8 rows.

Garter stitch stripe
Row 9 With ws facing, change to size 11 (8 mm)
   needles. K to end of row.
Row 10 Knit.
Knit 3 more rows = 13 rows.
From now on the main fabric is worked in reverse
   stockinette stitch. (Knit rows are worked with
   ws facing.)

Decreasing
Row 14 (Rs facing.) Dec 1 st at beginning of row by
   p2tog. P to end of row.
Row 15 (Ws facing.) Dec 1 st at beginning of row
   by k2tog. K to end of row = 54(60, 66) stitches.
Row 16 P.
Row 17 K.
Rpt rows 14 to 17 until a total of 6 sts each side
   has been decreased = 44(50, 56) sts.
Row 38 Work without any dec to row 42.

Increasing
Row 43 (Ws facing.) Inc 1 st each side by knitting
   into front and back of first st, k to last 2 sts,
   inc 1 st by knitting into front and back of next st,
   knit last remaining st = 46(52, 58) sts.
Rpt this every 4th row (rows 47, 51, 55 and 59) to
   inc 1 st at beginning and end of row until there are
   54(60, 66) sts on needle. Then work in reverse st.st
   to row 61.

Armhole shaping
Row 62 (Rs facing.) Bind off 3 sts purlwise,
   p to end.
Row 63 Bind off 3 sts knitwise, k to end.
Row 64 Bind off 2 sts purlwise, p to end.
Row 65 Bind off 2 sts knitwise, k to end.

Row 66 and Row 67 Rpt as for last 2 rows binding off 2 sts at beginning of each row. (7 sts dec each side = 40(46, 52) sts on needle.)
Work in reverse st.st as before for 32(36, 40) rows, to row 99(103, 107).
Bind off.

Front

Cast on 56(62, 68) sts using size 10½ (7 mm) needles and work rib as for Back.

Garter stitch stripe with center cable

(The center 10 stitches are purled on ws to produce the center cable panel.)

Row 9 (Ws facing.) Change to size 11 (8 mm) needles. Work as follows: k23(26, 29), p10, k23(26, 29).

Row 10 K to end.

Row 11 K23(26, 29), p10, k23(26, 29).

Row 12 K to end.

Row 13 K23(26, 29), p10, k23(26, 29).
From now on the base fabric is worked in reverse stockinette stitch. (Knit rows are worked with ws facing.) The center 10 stitches are worked for the cable.

Decreasing

Row 14 Dec 1 st at the beginning of row by p2tog, p21(24, 27), k10, p23(26, 29).

Row 15 Dec 1 st at beginning of row by k2tog, k21(24, 27), p10, k22(25, 28).
(You will dec 1 st at beginning of each row every 4 rows until 6 sts have been dec each side.)

Rows 16 and 17 Work in patt.

Rows 18 and 19 Dec 1 st at beginning of row each side.

Cable crossover patterning begins

Row 20 (Rs facing.) Cable row. P21(24, 27), sl next 5 sts onto cable needle knitwise and hold at front of work, k5, slip stitches off cable needle onto left-hand needle and k5, p21(24, 27).

Row 21 Continue as before in st patt (k21(24, 27), p10, k21(24, 27)).

Rows 22 and 23 Dec 1 st each side at beginning of row.
Continue working in patt and decreasing on rows 26/27, 30/31, 34/35 until six stitches have been decreased both sides, leaving 44(50, 56) sts.

Row 36 (Rs facing.) Cable row. P17(20, 23), sl 5 sts onto cable needle as before, k5, sl held sts onto left needle, k5, p17(20, 23).
Continue working in patt as before, without any decreasing, to row 42.

Increasing

Continue working in patt as before, increasing sts as directed.

Row 43 (Ws facing.) Inc 1 st each side by knitting into front and back of first st, work to last 2 sts, k into front and back of next st, k last st.
= 46(52, 58) sts.
Work 3 rows in patt without increasing.

Row 47 Inc 1 st each side = 48(54, 60) sts.
Work 3 rows in patt without increasing.
Row 51 Inc 1 st each side = 50(56, 62) sts.
Row 52 (Rs facing.) Cable row. P20(23, 26), cable
as before, p20(23, 26).
Work 2 rows in patt without increasing.
Row 55 Inc 1 sts at each side = 52(58, 64) sts.
Work 3 rows in patt without increasing.
Row 59 Inc 1 st each side = 54(60, 66) sts.
Work in patt to row 61.

Armhole shaping

Row 62 (Rs facing.) Bind off 3 sts purlwise, and
work in patt to end.
Row 63 Bind off 3 sts knitwise and work in patt to end.
Row 64 Bind off 2 sts purlwise and work in patt
to end.
Row 65 Bind off 2 sts knitwise and work in patt
to end.
Rows 67 and 68 Rpt as for last 2 rows, binding off
2 sts at beginning of each row. (7 sts dec each
side, 40(46, 52) sts on needle.)
Row 68 (Rs facing.) Cable row. P15(18, 21), cable as
before, p15(18, 21).
Row 69 K15(18 21), p10, k15(18, 21).

Neck shaping

Right side

Row 70 (Rs facing.) P13(16, 19), p2tog (to dec 1 st),
k5, then place all sts on left-hand needle on stitch
holder, then turn work (19(22, 25) sts). (You are now
working on shaping the right-hand side of your
garment.)
Row 71 P5, k14(17, 20).
Row 72 P4(17, 20), k5.
Row 73 P5, k14(17, 20).
Row 74 Neck shaping row. (Rs facing.) P12(15, 18),
p2tog, k5. Continue to work in patt, dec 1 st every
4 rows until 6(7, 8) sts have been decreased. (You
will dec 1 st on rows 78, 82, 86, 90, 94 and 98.)
Row 92(96, 100) P8(11, 14), k5. Then work without
decreasing until row 97(101, 105).
Row 98(102, 106) (Rs facing.) Bind off purlwise
7(10, 13) sts, k6. Continue to knit these 6 sts in
st.st for 12(14, 16) rows, then bind off. (This strip
will form half the back neck band.)

Left side

Transfer stitches from stitch holder onto left-hand
needle. Rejoin yarn. Work first row (row 70) as
follows:
Row 70 (Rs facing.) Neck shaping row. K5, p2tog,
p13(16, 19).
Row 71 14(17, 20), p5.
Continue to work as previously on right side,
decreasing 1 st every 4 rows, but this time using
the dec patt for left side of work.
Row 92(96, 100) K5, p8(11, 14). Then work without
decreasing until row 98(102, 106).
Row 99(103, 107) (Ws facing.) Bind off knitwise
7(10, 13) sts, then p6. Continue to knit these
6 sts in st.st for 12(14, 16) rows, then bind off.
(This has formed the other half of the back
neck band.)

Sleeves (knit two)

Cast on 26(32, 38) sts using size 10½ (7 mm)
needles.

Rib cuff

Work first row as follows. This will be the wrong
side of work.
Row 1 P3, (k2, p4), p last 3 sts.
Row 2 K3, (p2, k4), k last 3 sts.
These 2 rows form rib patt. Rpt 3 more
times = 8 rows.

Garter stitch stripe

Row 9 (Ws facing.) Change to size 11 (8 mm)
needles. K to end of row.
Row 10 K to end of row.
Rpt these 2 rows for 3 more rows.
Work in reverse st.st.
Row 14 With rs facing purl.
Row 15 K.
Continue in reverse stockinette stitch until row 27.
Row 28 (Rs facing.) Begin to shape sleeve. Inc 1 st
each side as follows:
P into front and back of first st, purl to last 2 sts,
purl into front and back of next stitch, p last st.
= 28(34, 40) sts.
Continue to work in reverse st.st and inc 1 st each
side as for row 28, every 18 rows. (Inc on rows 46
and 64.) 32(38, 44) sts on needle.)
Work in patt without shaping until row 78(82, 86).

Sleeve-head shaping

Row 82 Bind off 2 sts purlwise and p to end of row
= 30(36, 42) sts.

Row 83 Bind off 2 sts knitwise and k to end of row
= 28(34, 40) sts.

Row 84 Dec 1 st at beginning of row by p2 tog,
p to end of row = 27(33, 39) sts.

Row 85 Dec 1 st at beginning of row by k2 tog,
k to end of row = 26(32, 38) sts.

Rpt decreases of rows 84 and 85 until
16(22, 28) sts remain on needle.

Work to row 93(95, 97).

Row 94(96, 98) (Rs facing.) Bind off 2 sts
purlwise, p to end = 16(20, 24) sts.

Row 95(97, 99) Bind off 2 sts knitwise,
k to end = 14(18, 22)sts.

Row 96(98, 100) Bind off purlwise.

Assembly

Block and steam all garment pieces.
Sew in all ends to neaten.
Join shoulder seams using back stitch.
Join two strips from front neck
together using back stitch—this
will be the center back of the
neck. Then ease into place along
bound-off edge of back neck and
stitch using back stitch.
The seam of the neckband should
sit at the center back.
Attach sleeves to fit armholes and
join using back stitch, matching
center of sleeve head to
shoulder seam.
Join side seams using backstitch.

Double Cable Pattern

Once you have mastered this simple cable, you will be eager to experiment with different cable ideas. The 10 stitches that form the cable on this sweater can be worked in different cable patterns to vary the design. Pompoms or extra strips of cable can be added after knitting to enhance the texture of this garment, without making the cables difficult to knit.

Row 1 (Rs facing.) Purl as pattern, k4, p2, k4, p to end.

Row 2 (Ws facing.) Knit as pattern, p4, k2, p4, knit to end.

Repeat rows 1 and 2 to first cable row: (Rs row) purl as pattern, slip 2 sts onto cable needle, hold at back of work, k2, knit 2 sts from cable needle, p2, slip 2 sts onto cable needle, hold at front, k2, knit 2 st from cable needle, p to end. *

Repeat row 2.

Work rows 1 and 2 three times before next cable row.

*This cable is called C4B, p2, C4F.

Double cable pattern with threading detail

You can experiment with simple cabling to create more complex designs by threading strips of knit through the cable after the fabric has been knitted, like lacing shoes! Cast on three stitches and work in stockinette stitch to make a length two and a half times the length of your cables.

1 Starting at the bottom of the cable, tuck the end behind the first cable crossover and stitch to secure onto the wrong side of the knitting.

2 Weave the strip in and out of the cables to the top, zigzagging from left to right.

3 Double back, working down the cables and crossing to create a laced effect. Tuck the end behind the other bottom cable and stitch to secure on the wrong side. Adjust the strip to make sure that it lies evenly.

Single Rib Cable

This cable is worked in single rib for a flatter effect and then the optional pompoms have been added after knitting to create even more texture and stitch interest.

Adding textured pompoms

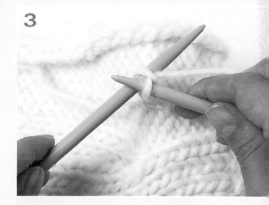

Row 1 (Rs facing.) Purl as pattern, k1, p1, k1, p1, k2, p1, k1, p1, k1, p to end.
Row 2 (Ws facing.) Knit as pattern, p1, k1, p1, k1, p2, k1, p1, k1, p1, k to end.
Repeat to first cable row.
With rs facing, purl as pattern, slip 5 stitches onto cable needle at front of work, k1, p1, k1, p1, k1. Slip stitches off cable needle onto left needle and k1, p1, k1, p1, k1, purl as pattern.
Repeat row 2.
Work rows 1 and 2 for 16 rows, repeat cable.

1 After knitting the main fabric, decide on the position of the bobbles, marking with pins or slip knot markers for accuracy. With the right side of the fabric (reverse stockinette stitch) facing you, push the needle up through two stitches in the position marked.

2 Remove the pin or marker and wrap the yarn around the tip of the needle, holding the working yarn and tail end securely. Drop the tail end and pull through, like knitting a stitch.

3 Knit into the stitch but do not slide it off left needle.

4 Bring yarn forward over needle and knit into stitch again and bring yarn forward in the same way. Knit stitch and slide off left needle. You have 5 stitches on needle. Purl all stitches.Knit all stitches.

5 Lift 4th stitch over 5th, using the tip of the right needle (as binding off). Repeat, lifting the 3rd, 2nd, and 1st stitches over 5th, leaving one stitch on the needle.

6 Cut yarn end and pull through the loop to fasten off. Thread the end through to the wrong side of main fabric, two rows above the original stitch. Thread the other yarn end through to wrong side, knot together, and sew in ends.

CHUNKY KNITS

Fair Isle

Fair Isle is the technique of working stockinette stitch with two colors in a row. Fair Isle patterns are usually worked from charts. The yarn not in use is carried across the back of the fabric. The floats of yarn can be stranded or woven in depending on how long they are.

Stranding

This method is suitable for carrying the yarn along for up to three stitches. Keeping one yarn up and the other yarn down means that your yarns should remain untangled at the end of each row.

On a knit row

1 Insert the right needle into the next stitch. Pick up the new B (pink) yarn in the right hand, take it over the A (black) yarn and knit required number of stitches.

2 Drop the B yarn and pick up the A yarn, taking it under the B yarn. Knit the required number of stitches. Continue in this way, keeping the stitches on the needles spread out so that the work does not gather up.

On a purl row

3 Insert the needle into the next stitch. Pick up the new B yarn in the right hand, take it over the A yarn and purl the required number of stitches.

4 Drop the B yarn and and pick up the A yarn, taking it under the B yarn. Purl the required number of stitches. Continue in this way.

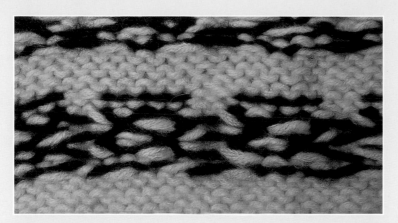

Weaving in

This method is used to carry a strand of yarn along more than three stitches. The float of yarn being carried is caught into the work every three or four stitches. You may find it easier to control the yarn being woven in with your left hand. Try to weave the yarn into different stitches on each row, to give an even finish

On a knit row

1 Knitting with the A yarn, insert the right needle into the next stitch as usual. Carry the B yarn under the A yarn and over the tip of the right needle.

2 Take the A yarn over the right needle as a usual knit stitch, but crossing the B yarn in front of the right needle. Lift the B yarn off the needle and knit the stitch through. Hold the B yarn down at the back of the work with the left hand and knit the next stitch as usual with the A yarn—the B yarn will be caught in.

On a purl row

3 Purling with the A yarn, insert the right needle into the next stitch as usual. Carry the B yarn under the A yarn and place over the tip of the right needle.

4 Take the A yarn over the needle as a usual purl stitch, but crossing the B yarn in front of the needle

5 Lift the B yarn off the needle and purl the stitch through. Hold the B yarn down with the left thumb and purl the next stitch with the A yarn—the B yarn will be caught in.

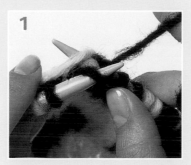

Intarsia

Intarsia is the term for knitting blocks of color from separate balls of yarn, without forming long floats behind the work. Intarsia can be worked with many different colors in one row. Before knitting, prepare the yarns that you will be using by counting the number of areas in each color and wind suitable lengths of yarn for each area onto bobbins. Work from whole balls for large areas.

Changing colors

To avoid holes in your knitting, the yarns are twisted around each other on the wrong side of the knitting as follows:

Knit row

1 Insert the end of needle into the next stitch. Place A (pink) yarn over B (black) yarn, and drop it so A is on the wrong side of the knitting.

2 Bring B yarn up and knit the stitch as usual.

Purl row

Insert right needle into next stitch. Place A yarn over new B yarn, and drop, so yarn A is toward you (on the wrong side of the knitting). Bring the B yarn up and purl the stitch.

Joining new color

1 Knitting in A, insert the right needle into the next stitch and, holding the tail of C in your left hand, lay the end of C (yellow) between the tips of the needles and across the A yarn.

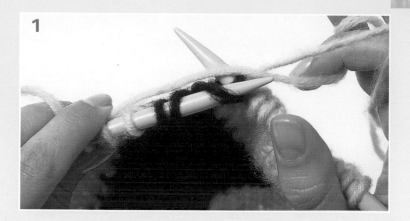

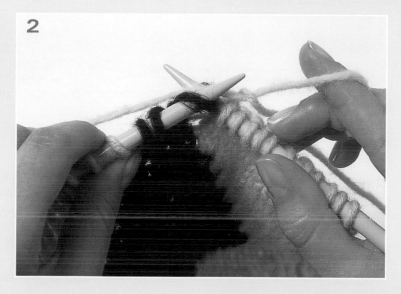

2 Place the working end of the C yarn (yellow) under the A and knit the stitch with it, dropping the tail off the needle as you do so.

3 (Back view) There are no floats on the back of the intarsia fabric. The tails of yarn can be woven in along the lines of color change when finishing the garment.

CHUNKY KNITS

PROJECT 11: Snowflake Style

An exaggerated adaptation of cozy Norwegian-style knits, Fair Isle designs have made a comeback on the catwalk, worn layered with eclectic patterns and lots of color. This adult-sized cardigan is bordered with snowflake patterning, and fastened with a chunky zipper. To get some experience of knitting Fair Isle, start with the Simple Ski Hat. There is no shaping to worry about in the Fair Isle band, allowing you to concentrate on new color-changing techniques.

SIMPLE SKI HAT

Materials
Extra chunky machine washable wool mix:
Color A—44 yds (40 m)
Color B—33 yds (30 m)
Color C—18 yds (16 m)
Color D—18 yds (16 m)
Size 10½ (7 mm) needles
Tapestry needle
Card discs for making pompom

Gauge
Over stockinette stitch on size 10½ (7 mm) needles: 13 sts and 16 rows to 4 in. (10 cm).

Abbreviations
st(s)–stitch(es); **k**–knit; **p**–purl; **st.st**–stockinette stitch; **k2tog**–knit 2 stitches together; **p2tog**–purl 2 stitches together; **rpt**–repeat; **rem**–remaining

To knit hat
Cast on 60 sts in color A on size 10½ (7 mm) needles.

Rib band
Work 2 rows in single rib in color A.
Work 8 rows single rib in color B.
Row 11 P one row.

Follow Fair Isle chart
(See pages 94–95 and 103).
Starting at row 1, stitch 1 of chart, work the 12-stitch Fair Isle design in stockinette stitch. Repeat the design 4 more times across the row.

Row 1 K row 1 of pattern.
Row 2 P row 2 of pattern.
Continue following the chart in stockinette stitch to row 15.
Row 16 P all stitches in color A.
Continue in A, working stockinette stitch to row 22.
Row 23 K2, k2tog, *(k6, k2tog)*. Rpt between ** 6 more times = 52 sts.
Row 24 *(p2tog, p5)*. Rpt between * and * 6 more times, p2tog, p1 = 44 sts.
Row 25 *(k2 tog, k4)*. Rpt between * and * 6 more times, k2tog = 36.
Row 26 *(p2tog, p3)*. Rpt between * and* 6 more times, p1 = 29 sts.
Row 27 *(k2, k2tog)*. Rpt between * and * 6 more times, k1 = 22 sts.
Row 28 P1, *(p2tog, p1) * Rpt between * and * 6 more times = 15 sts.
Row 29 *(k1, k2tog)*. Rpt between * and * 4 more times to end = 10 sts.

To fasten off
Break yarn leaving a tail of 8 in. (20 cm).
Thread tail into tapestry needle and pass through the remaining 10 stitches.

Remove knitting needle and use tail of yarn as
draw thread to gather up top of hat.
Gather up tightly and fasten off by sewing into
wrong side of hat.

Assembly

Join back seam with mattress stitch.
Sew in all ends to neaten.
Make a matching pompom (see page
105)
in colors C and D and sew to
top of hat.
Once you have mastered
Fair Isle with the ski
hat, you will feel
confident to make the
Snowflake Cardigan.

SNOWFLAKE CARDIGAN

Materials

Extra chunky machine washable wool mix
Color A—820(875, 930, 1010) yds [750(800,
850, 920) m]
Color B—205(220, 235, 255) yds [185(200,
215, 230) m]
Color C—83(88, 94, 101) yds [75(80, 85,
92) m]
Color D—83(88, 94, 101) yds [75(80,
85, 92) m
22 in. (55 cm) open-ended zipper
1 pair size 10½ (7 mm) needles
2 stitch holders
Tapestry needle
Sewing needle and strong thread to
sew zipper.
Tape measure

Finished measurements

Bust 38½(41, 43¼, 45¾) in. [98(104, 110,
116) cm]
Sleeve length 19(20, 20, 20½) in. [48(50,
50, 52) cm]
Length to back neck below neckband 25½(26,
26½, 27) in. [65(66, 67.5, 68.5) cm]

Gauge

Over stockinette stitch on size 10½ (7 mm)
needles: 13 sts and 16 rows to 4 in. (10 cm).

Abbreviations

(Same as for hat.)

To make cardigan

Start by knitting Front pieces, as rows may
have to be adjusted to fit zipper.

Left front

Cast on 31(33, 35, 37) sts in color B.
Work 2 rows single rib as given for Back.
Change to color A and work 6 rows in
single rib.

CHUNKY KNITS

Follow Fair Isle chart

Use the Fair Isle technique to knit the pattern on the chart in stockinette stitch.

Start pattern with a knit row at row 1, stitch 5, following the chart across to stitch 35(37, 39, 41).

Work to row 40 following main pattern.

Work to row 56, following dotty pattern established in rows 41–46.

Shaping

Continue working in dotty pattern throughout shaping.

Row 57 Bind off 2 sts at beginning of row, knit to end = 29(31, 33, 35) sts.

Row 58 P to last 2 sts, p2tog = 28(30, 32, 34) sts.

Row 59 Knit in pattern.

Continue in pattern to row 78 or until knitting measures 22 in. (55cm) (zipper length) finishing on a purl row.

NOTE If you adjust the number of rows knitted at this point, make a note and do the same adjustment for Back and other side of Front. See Adapting Patterns (page 126).

Row 79 K all sts.

Row 80 Put 5(5, 7, 9) sts on holder, p2tog, p to end = 22(24, 24, 24) sts.

Row 81 K to last 2 sts, k2tog = 21(23, 23, 23) sts.

Row 82 P2tog, p to end = 20(22, 22, 22) sts.

Row 83 K.

Continue in st.st to row 92(94, 96, 98).

Row 93(95, 97, 99) Bind off 7 sts knitwise, k to end = 13(15, 15, 15) sts.

Row 94(96, 98, 100) P to last 2 sts, p2tog = 12(14, 14, 14) sts.

Row 95(97, 99, 101) Bind off 6 sts knitwise, k to end = 6(8, 8, 8) sts.

Bind off rem 6(8, 8, 8) sts purlwise.

Right front

Cast on 31(33, 35, 37) sts in color B.

Work 2 rows single rib as given for Back.

Change to color A and work 6 rows in single rib.

Follow Fair Isle chart

Use the Fair Isle technique to knit the pattern on the chart in stockinette stitch.

Start pattern with a knit row at row 1, stitch 7(5, 3, 1), following the chart across to stitch 37.

Work rows as Back to row 56.

Shaping

Continue working in dotty pattern throughout shaping.

Row 57 K.

Row 58 Bind off 2 sts at beginning of row, purl to end = 29(31, 33, 35) sts.

Row 59 K to last 2 sts, k2tog = 28(30, 32, 34) sts.

Continue in pattern to row 78 or until knitting measures the same length as Left front finishing on a purl row.

Row 79 K5(5, 7, 9) sts and put on holder, k2tog, k to end = 22(24, 24, 24) sts.

Row 80 P to last 2 sts, p2tog = 21(23, 23, 23) sts.

Row 81 K2tog, k to end = 20(22, 22, 22) sts.

Row 82 P.

Continue in st.st to row 93(95, 97, 99).

Row 94(96, 98, 100) Bind off 7 sts purlwise, p to end = 13(15, 15, 15) sts.

Row 95(97, 99, 101) K to last 2 sts, k2tog = 12(14, 14, 14) sts.

Row 96(98, 100, 102) Bind off 6 sts purlwise, p to end = 6(8, 8, 8) sts.

Bind off rem 6(8, 8, 8) sts knitwise.

Back

In color B cast on 65(69, 73, 77) stitches.

Work in single rib:

Row 1 K1, (p1, k1) to end.

Row 2 P1, (k1, p1) to end.

Change to color A, continue in single rib working 6 rows (total 8 rows rib).

Follow Fair Isle chart

Work all in stockinette stitch.

Row 1 Follow chart in st.st, starting with a knit row at row 1, stitch 7(5, 3, 1) of chart to stitch 71(73, 75, 77).

Shaping

Continue working in dotty pattern
  throughout shaping.

Row 57 (K row.) Bind off 2 sts at
  beginning of row, k to end.

Row 58 (P row.) Bind off 2 sts at
beginning of row, p to last 2 sts, p2tog.

Row 59 K in pattern to last 2 sts, k2tog =
  59(63, 67, 71) sts.

Row 60 P. Continue in stockinette stitch to
  row 92(94, 96, 98).

Row 93(95, 97, 99) Bind off 7 stitches
  knitwise, knit next 14 sts, k2tog, put
  remaining 38(40, 44, 48) sts on holder.

Row 94(96, 98, 100) P2tog, p to last 2 sts,
  p2tog.

Row 95(97, 99, 101) Bind off 6 sts knitwise,
  knit remaining 5(7, 7, 7) sts.

Bind off remaining 5(7, 7, 7) sts.

Other side

Row 93(95, 97, 99) Leave 17(17, 21, 25)
  center neck sts on a stitch holder.

Pick up 23 sts, rs facing. Rejoin yarn and
  starting at neck, k2tog, k19(21, 21, 21).

Row 94 (96, 98, 100) Bind off 7 stitches
  purlwise, p to last 2 sts, p2tog.

Row 95 (97, 99, 100) K to last 2 sts, k2tog =
  11(13, 13, 13) sts.

Row 96 (98, 100, 102) Bind off 6 sts, p to end
  = 5(7, 7, 7) sts.

Bind off remaining 5(7, 7, 7) sts.

Sleeves (knit two)

Cast on 33(35, 37, 39) sts in color A.

Work 8 rows single rib

Row 1 K1, (p1, k1) to end.

Row 2 P1, (k1, p1) to end.

Row 9 Follow chart from row 17, stitch 23(22,
  21, 20) for patterning in st.st for 2 rows.

Start increasing

Take extra stitches into pattern.

Row 11 increase 1 st at both ends by knitting
  into front and back of sts.

Increase on every 2nd row as follows: rows 13,
  15, 17, 19, 21 and 23 = 47(49, 51, 53) sts.

Increase on every 4th row as follows: rows 27,
  31, 35, 39, 43, 47, 51, 55, 59, 63, 67 and 71 =
  71(73, 75, 77) sts.

Continue working in pattern to row 74(78, 78,
  80), or until work measures 19(20, 20, 20½)
  in. (48, 50, 50, 52 cm).

Bind off.

Finishing

Block and steam all pieces

Join both shoulder seams using mattress
  stitch.

Collarband

Leave 5(5, 7, 9) sts each on left and right
  fronts on stitch holders.

In color A pick up 55(57, 63, 69) sts for
  collar evenly around neck.

Row 1 Work single rib, k1, p1 across
  55(57, 63, 69) sts. At end of row, p into
  first st on stitch holder, leave (4, 4, 6, 8)
  sts on holder.

Row 2 Turn and work back. K1, p1 across
  56(58, 64, 70) sts. At end of row knit into
  first st from stitch holder.

**CHUNKY
KNITS**

Row 3 Work in single rib (p1, k1) across all 57(59, 65, 71) sts. At end of row work into next 2 sts from stitch holder.

Row 4 Work in single rib across all 59(61, 67, 73) sts and work into next 2 sts on stitch holder.

Rpt rows 3 and 4, picking up all stitches from holders = total 65(67, 77, 83) sts.

Bind off ribwise.

Front band

NOTE It is important to get the length of the front band correct. You can get the most accurate gauge for your rib knitting by measuring the rib on the back piece. Measure the center front length up from the bottom of the rib to the last row of stockinette stitch. Measure the same distance across the cast-on edge of the rib on the back piece, when gently stretched, and count the stitches.

Using yarn A, evenly pick up the required number of stitches by knitting into the edge of the left front. (See Picking up Stitches.)

Work one row single rib.

Bind off ribwise.

Repeat for right front.

Position sleeves, matching shoulder seam with center of sleeve bound-off edge. Check that the sleeves reach the same row of pattern on back and front. Join using mattress stitch.

Sew side seams and sleeve seams with mattress stitch. Sew in all ends.

Insert zipper following instructions on page 70.

Reading a chart

Patterns for color knitting, like Fair Isle and Intarsia, are often given in the form of a chart. Each square of the chart represents a different stitch. The squares are filled with different colors or symbols to represent the yarn color that should be used.

The chart is followed from bottom to top starting at the bottom right on a right side row. The right side/knit rows are numbered at the right of the chart and read from right to left and the wrong side/purl rows are numbered at the left of the chart and read from left to right.

The chart for the hat has a 12-stitch repeat; therefore the pattern is repeated across the row. The chart for the cardigan shows at the full width of the back and different areas are indicated for working the fronts and the sleeves.

A chart gives a clear indication of the pattern to be produced and is easy to follow. It is fun to chart up a pattern of your own using squared paper, but allow for the fact that a knitted stitch is usually wider than it is tall, so the pattern on the chart will appear wider and shorter when knitted.

Simple ski hat

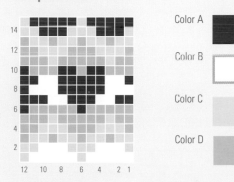

Color A	■
Color B	□
Color C	▨
Color D	▦

Snowflake cardigan

Two-Color Ribbing

Two-color ribbing works well as an alternative trim to Fair Isle garments. You will use the stranding technique (see Fair Isle Techniques), passing yarns across the back of the work, while working the rib.

Adapting the Pattern Width
You will need a multiple of 4 stitches plus 2, to work this double rib correctly, so you may need to adjust patterns accordingly. For example, for second size of the Snowflake cardigan adjust as follows:

For the Back Cast on 70 sts for rib and knit the first two stitches together at the beginning of the last row of rib.
For Front Cast on 30 stitches for rib and knit twice into the first and last stitch on the last row of rib.
For Sleeves Cast on 34 stitches and knit twice into the first stitch on the last row of rib.

Working the Two-color Rib
Cast on in Yarn A. In order to keep all floats on the wrong side of the fabric you need to make sure that the yarns are always left at the back of the work before a color change.
Row 1 (Rs facing.) K2B, (p2A, k2B) to end.

1 Keep the B yarn to the back after knitting, before bringing the A yarn forward to purl.

2 Take the A yarn back after purling, before knitting with the B yarn.

Row 2 (Ws facing.) P2A, (k2B, p2A) to end
Bring the B yarn forward after knitting, before purling with the A yarn. Repeat rows 1 and 2 to required length of rib.

Making Pompoms

Pompoms are easy to make and are a fun way of using up leftover yarns You can experiment with striping and mixing different colors and yarns together. Ready-made pompom discs are available to buy, but they are really easy to make in any size, using card from empty cereal boxes or old greetings cards.

Making the discs

Cut two discs of card slightly bigger than the diameter of the pompom size required. Cut a circular hole in the middle of each disc about half the diameter or a little less. If the hole is too big the pompom will be distorted. If too small, the pompom will not be fat enough.

Making the Pompom

Wind off some yarn, or use balls of yarn small enough to fit through the hole.

1 Hold both the discs together and wind the yarn around the ring until it is completely covered.

2 Wind more layers of yarn until the hole is too small to continue and cut the yarn.

3 Take a sharp pair of scissors and cut the yarn right around the edge, pushing the blade between the discs. Hold the discs firmly in the other hand.

4 Separate the discs by a half inch or so (1–2 cm), and tie a length of strong yarn between them, tightly around the middle of the pompom. Leave this yarn end long so you can use it to stitch the pompom in place.

5 Remove the discs and smooth out the pompom, trimming any untidy ends.

CHUNKY KNITS

CHUNKY KNITS

PROJECT 12: Man's Intarsia Sweater

This oversized V-necked sweater is a chunky update of a traditional Argyle design. The geometric diamond patterning, followed from a chart, is a good first intarsia project as the patterning repeats across the row. The back is kept plain and simple for maximum contrast, but if you wish to continue the patterned border to the back, just follow the instructions for the front to the armhole shaping and double the amount of color A and B yarns required.

Materials

Super chunky wool yarn:
Color A—30(39) oz [850(1100) g]
Color B—3(4) oz [80(100) g]
Color C—3(4) oz [80(100) g]
1 pair size 17 (12 mm) needles
Tapestry needle
16(20) bobbins

Gauge

Over stockinette stitch on size 17 (12 mm) needles:
   8 sts and 12 rows to 4 in. (10 cm)

Finished measurements

Back length 26¾(29½) in. [68(75) cm]
Chest at underarm 50(54) in. [125(137) cm]
Sleeve seam length 19¾(21) in. [50(53) cm]

Abbreviations

st(s)–stitch(es); **k**–knit; **p**–purl; **st.st**–stockinette stitch; **m1**–make one stitch; **beg**–beginning; **dec**–decrease; **rh**–right hand; **rem**–remaining; **sl1, k1, psso**–slip one, knit one, pass slip stitch over; **rpt**–repeat; **rs**–right side; **ws**–wrong side; **inc**–increase; **k2tog**–knit 2 stitches together; **p2tog**–purl 2 stitches together; **tbl**–through back of loops

Back

Cast on 51(63) sts in color A.

Rib

Row 1 P1, k2 * (p2, k2) repeat from * to end.
Row 2 *(P2, k2) rep from * to last 3 sts, p2, k1.
Repeat rows 1 and 2 for 6 more rows.

Stockinette stitch

Row 1 Rs facing, k to end.
Row 2 Purl.
Continue in st.st until work measures 15¾(17) in. [40(43) cm] ending with a ws row.

Armhole shaping

Row 1 Bind off 3(4) sts at beg row, k to end = 48(59) sts.
Row 2 Bind off 3(4) sts at beg row, p to end = 45(55) sts.
Row 3 Dec 1 st at each end of row = 43(53) sts.
Row 4 Dec 1 st at each end of row = 41(51) sts.
Row 5 Dec 1 st at each end of row = 39(49) sts.
Continue working in stockinette stitch without shaping until armhole measures 10¾(12½) in. [27(32) cm], ending with a ws row.

Shoulder and back neck shaping

Right side

Bind off 5(7) sts at beg of next row, knit until there are 5(7) sts on rh needle. Put rem 29(35) sts onto a st holder.
Next row, purl 5(7) sts.
Bind off all 5(7) sts.
Slip stitches from st holder onto left needle. With rs facing, rejoin yarn and bind off 19(21) sts for neck opening, k to end.

Left side

Bind off 5(7) sts at beg row, purl to end = 5(7) sts.
Next row, knit all sts.
Bind off all 5(7) sts.

Front

The multicolored diamond pattern is worked using the intarsia technique (see pages 96–97). Cast on 51(63) sts in color A and work rib as back.

Intarsia pattern

Wind off 4(5) bobbins of color A, 4(5) bobbins of color B, and 8(10) bobbins of color C.

Starting with a rs row at bottom right-hand side of chart (row1, st1), work rows 1 and 2 in color A from main ball.

Continue following the chart using the bobbins of yarn, working 4(5) diamonds to row 25. The final stitch on each row should be worked in color A.

Rejoin main ball of yarn in color A. Continue to work in st.st in main yarn until the work measures 15¾(17) in. [40(43) cm], ending on a ws row (work number of rows to match the Back).

Armhole shaping

Row 1 Bind off 3(4) sts at beg row, k to end = 48(59) sts.

Row 2 Bind off 3(4) sts at beg row, p to end = 45(55) sts.

■ Color A
■ Color B
□ Color C

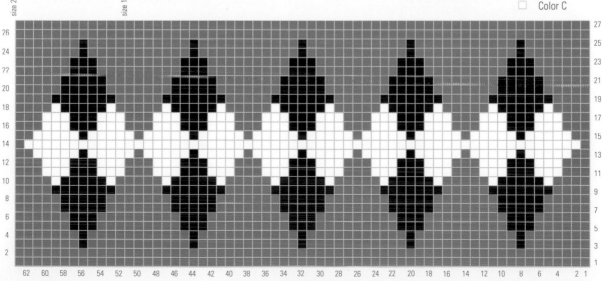

CHUNKY KNITS

Row 3 Dec 1 st at each end of row = 43(53) sts.
Row 4 Dec 1 st at each end of row = 41(51) sts.
Row 5 Dec 1 st at each end of row = 39(49) sts.
Row 6 Purl all sts.

Left V-neck shaping
Row 1 K18(22), k2tog. Put rem 19(23) sts onto a
st holder for right side.
Row 2 P.
Row 3 K to last 3 st, k2tog, k1 = 18(23) sts.
Row 4 P.
Repeat rows 3 and 4, for neck shaping, to row
18(20), when 11(15) sts rem.
Row 19(21) K.
Row 20(22) P.
Row 21(23) K to last 3 sts, k2tog, k1 = 10(14) sts.
Row 22(24) P.
Continue in st.st until armhole measures
10¾(12½) in. [27(32) cm], ending on a ws row.

Left shoulder shaping
Bind off 5(7) sts at beg row, k to end.
Next row, p5(7) sts.
Bind off all 5(7) sts.

Right V-neck shaping
Slip all 19(23) sts on st holder onto needle for
right neck.
Rejoin yarn at center front.
Row 1 K.
Row 2 P.
Row 3 K1, sl1, k1, psso, knit to end = 18(22) sts.
Row 4 P.
Rpt rows 3 and 4, for neck shaping, to row 18(20),
when 11(15) st rem.
Row 19(21) K.
Row 20(22) P.
Row 21(23) K1, sl1, k1, psso, knit to end
= 10(14) sts.
Row 22(24) P.
Continue in st.st until armhole measures
10¾ (12½) in. [27(32) cm], ending on a ws row.
(Rs facing.) Knit 1 row.

Right shoulder shaping
Bind off 5(7) sts at beg row, purl to end.
Next row, k5(7) sts.
Bind off all 5(7) sts.

Sleeves (knit two)
Cast on 26(30) sts with color A.

Rib
Row 1 K2, * (p2, k2) rep from * to end.
Row 2 P2 * (k2, p2) rep from * to end.
Rpt rows 1 and 2 for 6 more rows to row 8.

Stockinette stitch
Row 1 (Rs facing.) K.
Row 2 P.
Row 3 Inc 1 st at both ends = 28(32) sts.
Continue in stockinette stitch increasing as for row
3 on every 6th row until row 39(46) = 40(46) sts.
(Rows 9, 15, 21, 27, 33, 39(46).)
Work 3 rows, then increase at both ends on row
43(49) = 42(48) sts.
Continue working in st.st without shaping until
work measures 19¾(21) in. [50(53) cm], ending
with a ws row.

Sleeve-head shaping
Row 1 Bind off 3(4) sts, k to end = 39(44) sts.
Row 2 Bind off 3(4) sts, p to end = 36(40) sts.
Row 3 K1, sl1, k1, psso. K to last 3 sts, k2tog, k1
= 34(38) sts.
Row 4 P.
Row 5 K1, sl1, k1 psso. K to last 3 sts, k2tog, k1
= 32(36) sts.

Smaller size only
Row 6 P1, p2tog, p to last 3 sts, p2togtbl, p1
= 30 sts.

Larger size only
Row 6 K.
Row 7 K1, sl1, k1 psso. K to last 3 sts, k2tog, k1
= (34) sts.

Both sizes
Bind off all stitches.

Assembly
Block and steam all pieces.
Sew both shoulder seams using mattress stitch.

V-neck rib trim
Left side
Using color A and with rs facing, Knit up 18(21) sts
  from center front point of V to left shoulder, and
  10(11) sts from left shoulder to center back
  = 28(32) sts.
Row 1 (Ws facing.) * (K2, p2) rep from * to end.
Row 2 Rpt row 1 in color A.
Change to color C. Rpt rows 1 and 2.
Change to color B. Rpt rows 1 and 2.
Bind off all sts.

Right side
(Rs facing.) Using color A, knit up
  10(11) sts from center back neck
  to right shoulder seam, 18(21)
  sts from right shoulder seam
  to center front point of V
  = 28(32) sts.
Rpt 6 rows as for left side and
  bind off.
Stitch ends of rib neck in
  place using mattress
  stitch, overlapping at
  front point of V, and
  matching stitches at
  center back.
Stitch sleeves into place
  and join side seams
  and sleeve seams.
Weave in all loose ends
  to neaten.

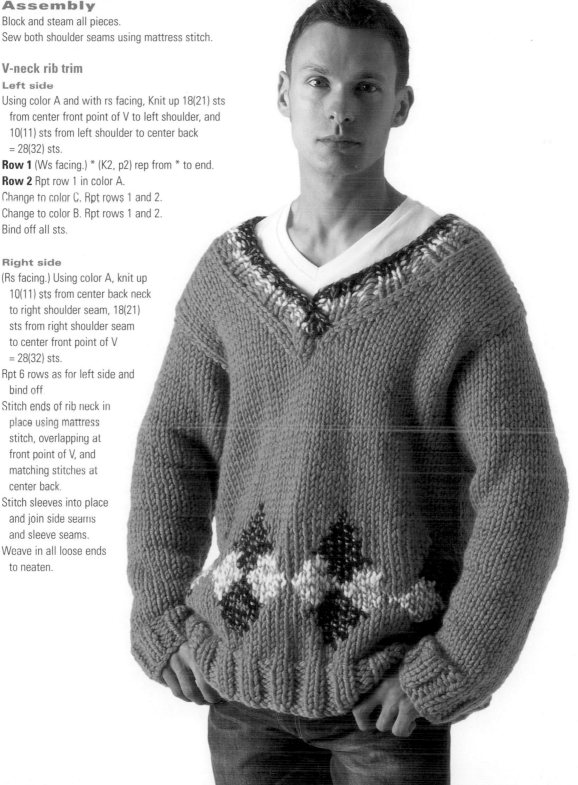

Bobbins and Balls

The intarsia technique requires you to work with several balls or bobbins of color in a row. It is important to prepare the yarns carefully and to keep organized in order to avoid tangled ends. Only unwind a short length of yarn from the ball or bobbin at a time. When following a chart, color identification can be made easier by labeling each ball or bobbin with the yarn color—A, B, etc.

Before starting the intarsia pattern, wind the yarn required for small- to medium-sized areas around bobbins. Balls of yarn used for larger areas of color can be prepared by placing each ball in a clear plastic bag, secured with an elastic band so that the yarn can be pulled through easily. This will help to avoid tangles if dealing with several balls of yarn at once.

Sewing in Ends

Intarsia creates lots of loose ends on the wrong side of the fabric. The ends need to be neatened as usual before joining the seams (see page 29). Ends should be woven in along lines of color change, where possible, or into knitting of the same color. If you are working with many yarn ends, it is advisable to sew yarn ends in after every 10–15 rows, in order to avoid tangles and a laborious job at the end.

  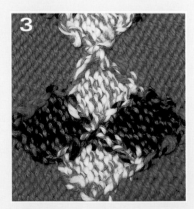

1 Weave ends in on the wrong side of the fabric, working along the outlines of areas of the same color.

2 Weave the yarn back on itself and stretch the knitting gently so that the woven-in yarn is not stitched too tightly into place, as this may distort the fabric.

3 Trim the loose ends to leave a neat finish.

Swiss Darning

Swiss darning is a useful embroidery technique that duplicates a knitted stitch. It is a simple way of adding areas or lines of different color to any design and can be used to embellish or correct an intarsia or Fair Isle design once it has been knitted. If you wish to use swiss darning to create more pattern or add color to a design, photocopy the original intarsia chart and draw in the stitches to be worked before you add the embroidery to the knitted fabric.

1 Insert the needle from the wrong side of the fabric through the base of the knitted stitch and take the needle behind the "V" of the stitch above. Leave a tail of yarn on the wrong side of the fabric, long enough to be woven in later.

2 From the right side, insert the needle through the knitting at the base of the stitch again and pull the yarn through. A new V-shaped stitch now covers the original.

3 Bring the needle through to the right side at the base of the next stitch to be covered.

4 Repeat the process for each stitch to be covered and finish off by weaving in the loose ends on the wrong side of the fabric to secure.

CHUNKY KNITS

Embellishing Techniques

It can be exciting to combine different materials and colors into knitting, creating pattern and surface interest. Decorative embellishment such as the addition of beads or sequins can be worked into designs as you are knitting, or embroidery can be added to work after it has been knitted. It is always advisable to test beads or embroidery on a sample of the fabric that you will be knitting, to be sure that the knit will not get distorted and also to refine your technique for a professional result.

Beads and sequins

Beads and sequins can be easily knitted into your work adding a highly decorative dimension to knitted fabric. You can knit beads in for an all-over texture, or place as a motif or border. When knitting beads into chunky knits, the slipstitch method shown here is the most useful, as it can be used for large-sized beads.

Choosing beads

With chunky yarns it is particularly important to check that the holes in the beads or sequins are big enough to fit a double thickness of the yarn that you are using. If the beads are too small they will slip through the stitches to the wrong side of the fabric, especially if it is not very tightly knitted. Also check that the weight of the beads is not too heavy for the fabric, and that the cleaning instructions for beads and yarn are compatible.

Threading

Beads or sequins must be threaded onto the yarn before being knitted into the work. To avoid having to break the yarn, it is always safer to over-estimate the amount of beads that you think you will need. If you do run out of beads before the end of a ball, break the yarn at the beginning of a row and weave in the ends as usual, or unwind the ball and thread more beads from the other end.

You may be able to use a large-eyed sewing needle to thread the required number of beads onto the yarn. Make sure that the needle can pass through the beads easily. With chunky beads this is usually the easiest way to thread but, if you do not have a suitable needle, you can thread as follows:

1 Fold a length of sewing cotton in half and pass both the ends through a needle that is fine enough to fit through the bead.

2 Thread the end of the yarn through the loop in the sewing thread and fold it back on itself.

3 Pass the sewing needle through the beads and pull the yarn through. If you are using differently colored or sized beads remember that the last beads that you thread on will be the first that you knit with, so be sure to thread beads in the correct order.

Knitting beads and sequins into work

This technique is best worked on a knit row on the right side. Remember to thread the beads onto the yarn before you start knitting.

1 On a right side row, knit to the position of the stitch to be beaded and bring the yarn forward to the front of the work (as if to purl). Bring the next bead up the yarn so that it is close to the knitting.

2 Slip the next stitch purlwise by inserting the right needle into the stitch from back to front and moving it onto the right needle without working into it.

3 Push the bead right up, so that it is touching the knitting and take the yarn to the back so that the bead is suspended in front of the slipped stitch.

Knit the next stitch as usual. You will see that the bead is held in place in front of the slipped stitch.

You can continue across the row until you come to the position of the next bead.

If the bead that you are using is very large or long, you may need to slip two or more stitches together to make room for it. All slipped stitches are worked into as normal on the next row.

CHUNKY KNITS

Embroidery

Embroidery is an effective way of adding decorative detail and color to your work. Many embroidery stitches can be worked successfully onto knitting; combining different color and stitches can give limitless possibilities for adding original or traditional decorative patterning to knitwear. Embroidery can be used to add color and texture to knitted stitch patterns or as a decorative motif.

It is always easier to work with a yarn of similar type and thickness to main yarn, although mixing yarn qualities can also be very effective if worked carefully.

It is usually advisable to embroider the fabric after all pieces have been knitted but before sewing up.

Use a large blunt sewing needle to avoid splitting stitches.

Always work with the right side of the knitting facing you and begin by weaving in the yarn end on the wrong side before bringing the needle through to the right side, pulling the yarn through.

Stem stitch

This stitch is useful for creating a straight or curved line of stitches. It is usually worked from left to right.

Bring the thread to the front of the work. Take the needle along to the right, push into the knitting and through to the right side again, from right to left, bringing the thread through half way along the first stitch made. Repeat this process to create a line of stitches.

Satin stitch

This stitch is good for making small solid shapes of color. It is best worked in a smooth, fat yarn, for good coverage. The stitches are usually worked horizontally, in line with the rows of knitting

Bring the thread through to the front of the work. Take the needle along to the right, push into the knitting and through to the front of the work again, coming out just below the last stitch made. Make more stitches in the same way, each time working close to the stitch above so that the stitches fully cover the area being embroidered.

Lazy daisy

This decorative flower is made of five or more petals, each made from a loop of yarn, which is stitched in place. The daisies work well scattered over a fabric or worked as a motif or border.

1 Work each petal from the center of the flower. Bring the needle and yarn through to the right side and pass the needle back into the same place, leaving a loop of yarn for the petal. Bring the needle back through to the right side at the tip of the petal and make a small stitch over the petal loop, catching it in place.

2 Bring the yarn back through to the center point and repeat for each petal.

Chain stitch with crochet hook

Chain stitch can be worked into knitting with a crochet hook. This is faster and neater than using a sewing needle. The crochet hook should be about the same size or a little smaller than the needles used to knit the fabric.

1 Hold the crochet hook above the fabric and hold the yarn underneath the fabric with the other hand. Push the hook down through the knitting and catch the yarn beneath. Pull a loop of the yarn through to the right side of the knitting.

2 Insert the hook down into the next stitch and pull up a second loop so that you have two loops on the hook.

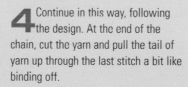

3 Draw the second loop through the first, making the first chain stitch.

4 Continue in this way, following the design. At the end of the chain, cut the yarn and pull the tail of yarn up through the last stitch a bit like binding off.

5 Use the crochet hook from the wrong side of the fabric to draw the yarn through catching the end of the chain into place

6 Using the crochet hook, and working from the wrong side of the fabric, draw the end of the yarn in and out of the back of the chain stitches to secure.

PROJECT 13: Beaded Sweater

This slim fitted winter sweater is knitted in super chunky yarn and features a deep turtleneck collar embellished with multicolor beading. More beads are worked into the eyelet detailing at the cuffs and, if you want to make even more of an impact, try experimenting with decorative beaded edging or embroidery ideas.

Materials

700(700, 700, 790) yds [640(640, 640, 720)m] super chunky wool yarn
171(171, 178, 186) beads with holes large enough for yarn to thread through
1 pair size 17 (12 mm) needles
Large-eyed tapestry needle

Gauge

Over stockinette stitch on size 17 (12 mm) needles:
8 sts and 12 rows to 4 in. (10 cm)

Finished measurements

Center back length 20½(20¾, 21, 22¼) in.
[52(53, 53, 56.5) cm]
Bust at underarm 34(36, 38, 40) in.
[86(91, 96, 102) cm]
Sleeve seam length 16(16, 16½, 16½) in.
[41(41, 42, 42) cm]

Abbreviations

st(s)–stitch(es); **k**–knit; **p**–purl; **st.st**–stockinette stitch; **inc**–increase; **beg**–beginning; **sl1, k1, psso**–slip one, knit one, pass slip stitch over; **k2tog**–knit 2 stitches together; **p2tog**–purl 2 stitches together; **rs**–right side; **ws**–wrong side; **rem**–remaining; **yf**–bring yarn forward; **dec**–decrease; **rpt**–repeat; **tbl**–through back of loops

Back

Cast on 29(31, 33, 35) sts in super chunky yarn on size 17 (12 mm) needles using cable cast-on method.
Work in stockinette stitch throughout as follows:
Row 1 (Rs facing .) K.
Row 2 P.
Continue to row 10(10, 10, 12).

Side shaping

Row 11(11, 11, 13) Inc 1 st at beg and end of row =
31(33, 35, 37) sts.
Continue in st.st to row 18(18, 18, 20).
Row 19(19, 19, 21) Inc 1 st at beg and end of row =
33(35, 37, 39) sts.
Continue in st.st to row 26(26, 26, 28).
Row 27(27, 27, 29) Inc 1 st at beg and end of row =
35(37, 39, 41) sts.
Continue in st.st until work measures 12½(12½, 12½, 13½) in. [32(32, 32, 34) cm], ending on a ws row.

Armhole shaping

Row 1 Bind off 1(2, 2, 3) sts, k to end
= 34(35, 37, 38) sts.
Row 2 Bind off 1(2, 2, 3) sts, p to end
= 33(33, 35, 35) sts.
Row 3 Sl1, k1, psso, k to last 2 sts, k2tog
= 31(31, 33, 33) sts.
Row 4 P2tog, p to last 2 sts, p2togtbl
= 29(29, 31, 31) sts.
Row 5 Sl1, k1, psso, k to last 2 sts, k2tog
= 27(27, 29, 29) sts.
Continue working in st.st, until armhole measures 8(8¼, 8½, 8¾) in. [20.5(21, 21.5, 22) cm], ending on a ws row.

Back neck and shoulder shaping

Right side

Row 1 (Rs facing.) Bind off 3 sts at shoulder, knit until there are 7(7, 7, 7) sts on right-hand needle and put remaining 17(17, 19, 19) sts onto a stitch holder.
Row 2 (Ws facing.) Bind off 3(3, 3, 3) sts at neck edge and purl to end.
Bind off rem 4 sts.

Left side

Slip 10(10, 10, 10) sts from holder onto needle, leave rem 7(7, 9, 9) sts on holder for neck.

Row 1 (Rs facing.) Rejoin yarn at neck edge and knit to end.

Row 2 (Ws facing.) bind off 3 sts at shoulder and purl to end.

Row 3 Bind off 3(3, 3, 3) sts at neck edge and knit 4.

Bind off rem 4 sts.

Front

Work as for Back until work measures 12¼(12¼, 12½, 13½) in. [32(32, 32, 34) cm], ending on a ws row.

Armhole shaping

Row 1 Bind off 1(2, 2, 3) sts, k to end = 34(35, 37, 38) sts.

Row 2 Bind off 1(2, 2, 3) sts, p to end = 33(33, 35, 35) sts.

Row 3 Sl1, k1, psso, k to last 2 sts, k2tog = 31(31, 33, 33) sts.

Row 4 P2tog, p to last 2 sts, p2togtbl = 29(29, 31, 31) sts.

Row 5 Sl1, k1, psso, k to last 2 sts, k2tog = 27(27, 29, 29) sts.

Continue working in stockinette stitch, until armhole measures 6(6¼, 6½, 6¾) in. [15(16, 16.5, 17) cm], ending on a ws row.

Front neck and shoulder shaping

Left neck shaping

Row 1 (Rs facing.) K10(10, 10, 10), put rem 17(17, 19, 19) sts onto stitch holder.

Row 2 (Ws facing.) P2tog at neck edge, p to end = 9(9, 9, 9) sts.

Row 3 K to last 2 sts, k2tog = 8(8, 8, 8) sts.

Row 4 P.

Row 5 K to last 2 sts, k2tog = 7(7, 7, 7) sts.

Row 6 P.

Left shoulder shaping

Row 1 Bind off 3(3, 3, 3) sts, k to end = 4 sts.

Row 2 P.

Bind off rem 4 sts.

CHUNKY KNITS

Right neck shaping

Slip 10(10, 10, 10) sts from st holder onto needle.
Leave rem 7(7, 9, 9) sts for neck.
(Rs Facing.) Rejoin yarn at neck edge and
k 10(10, 10, 10).
Row 2 P to last 2 sts, p2tog at neck edge
= 9(9, 9, 9) sts.
Row 3 K2tog, k to end = 8(8, 8, 8) sts.
Row 4 P.
Row 5 K2tog, k to end = 7(7, 7, 7) sts.
Row 6 P.

Right shoulder shaping

Row 1 K to end.
Row 2 Bind off 3(3, 3, 3) sts, p to end = 4 sts.
Row 3 K.
Bind off rem 4 sts.

Sleeves (knit two)

Before knitting each sleeve, thread 40(40, 40, 44)
beads onto yarn (see page 112).

Beaded lace cuffs

(See page 120.)
Cast on 23(23, 23, 25) sts on size 17 (12 mm)
needles.
Row 1 K.
Row 2 (Ws facing.) K1, * (k2tog, yf with bead)
repeat from * to last 2 sts, k2.
Repeat these two rows three more times = 8 rows.
(Rs facing.) Starting with a knit row, work 8 rows
st.st = 16 rows.

Increasing

Row 17 (Rs facing.) Inc 1st at beginning and end of
row = 25(25, 25, 27) sts.
Continue in st.st increasing at both ends of every
12th row as follows:
Row 29 Inc 1 st at beg and end of row = 27(27, 27,
29) sts.
Row 41 Inc 1 st at beg and end of row = 29(29, 29,
31) sts.
Continue in st.st until work measures 16(16, 16½,
16½) in. [41(41, 42, 42) cm], ending with a rs row.

Sleeve-head shaping

Work in st.st throughout.
Row 1 (Rs facing.) Bind off 1(2, 2, 3) sts at beg row.

Row 2 Bind off 1(2, 2, 3) sts at beg row = 27(25, 25,
25) sts.
Row 3 Dec 1 st at beg and end of row = 25(23, 23,
23) sts.
Row 4 Knit without decreasing.
Row 5 Dec 1 st at beg and end of row = 23(21, 21,
21) sts.
Row 6 Knit without decreasing.
Row 7 Purl, dec 1(0, 0, 0) st at beg and end of row.
Row 8 Knit without decreasing.
Row 9 Dec 1 st at beg and end of row = 19(19, 19,
19) sts.
Row 10 Work without decreasing.
Repeat rows 9 and 10 3(3, 3, 3) more times = 13 sts.
Row 17 Dec 1 st at beg and end of row
= 11 sts.
Row 18 Dec 1 st at beg and end of row = 9 sts.
Bind off all stitches.

Assembly

Block all pieces.
Using mattress stitch and working half a stitch from
the edge, join the right shoulder seam.

Collar

With rs facing and using size 17 (12 mm) needles,
pick up and knit 7(7, 7, 7) sts down front-left side
of neck, 7(7, 9, 9) sts from holder at front, 7 sts up
front-right side of neck, 5 sts from back-right side
of neck, 7(7, 9, 9) sts from back holder, 6(6, 5, 5)
sts up back-left side of neck = 39(39, 42, 42) sts.
Row 1 Knit twice into first stitch, * p1, k2, rpt from
* to last 2 sts, p1, k1 = 40(40, 43, 43) sts
Row 2 P1, k1, ** p2, k1, repeat from ** to last
2 sts, p2.
Continue in (2 x 1) rib as established, to row 16.
Break yarn and thread 91(91, 98, 98) beads.

Beading using slipstitch method

(See page 113.)
Row 17 * K2, yf with bead, sl1. Rpt from * to
last st, k1.
Row 18 P.
Rpt rows 17 and 18 five more times.
Row 29 * K2, yf with bead, sl1. Rpt from * to
last st, k.
Bind off purlwise, loosely.

Joining seams

Use mattress stitch, working half a stitch in from the
  side edges for all seams.

Join left shoulder seam.

Join collar seam, reversing seam for collar fold over
  (see page 47).

Set in sleeves, matching center of sleeve head to
  shoulder seam, and ease to fit armholes.

Join side and sleeve seams.

Sew in all ends to neaten.

Variations

If you wish to add even more
beads to the sweater, try using the
crochet beaded trim idea shown
on the next page. This can be
worked around the bottom edge of
the garment or as an extra trim to
the collar.

To create focus on the beaded
collar, the sleeves can be kept
plain. Simply cast on the same
number of stitches and work the
first eight rows in stockinette
stitch, starting with a knit row.

Beading Techniques

Although the slipstitch technique (see page 113) is the most commonly used method of beading knitting, beading can also be added to textured stitch patterns to create exciting new fabric structures. The beads will add weight and affect the behavior of the finished fabric, so they are often best placed as trims and borders. With chunky yarn, the lace holes and beads are clearly defined and easy to work with, so you can experiment with adding beads to different stitch patterns on areas of garments. Beads can also be added to finished pieces of knitting using simple crochet techniques or they can be stitched into place with a large-eyed, blunt-ended tapestry needle.

Beaded lace holes

With this technique, the beading is worked on a wrong-side row and the beads end up on the right side when the next row is worked. The required amount of beads should be threaded onto the yarn before the beaded knitting is started (see page 112). The first stitch of the row is worked without a pattern, to allow for the seam to be sewn.

1 Bring the yarn forward (yf) and push the bead along the yarn so that it is close to the right-hand needle.

2 Insert the right needle into the next two stitches knitwise, wrap the yarn round the needle counterclockwise, and knit both stitches together (k2tog).

3 The bead sits on the yarnover strand that has been made between the knitted stitches on the right-hand needle.

4 Repeat steps 1 and 2 across the row. The row of beads should be on the wrong side of the fabric and the original amount of stitches should remain on the needle.

5 On the right-side row, knit into each stitch and yarnover strand as usual. The beads will come to sit on the yarnover strand on the right side of the fabric as the row is knitted.

Crochet beaded edge

This beading technique can be applied to the edge of any knitted fabric, using the same yarn and a crochet hook in a suitable size for the yarn being used. The same process can also be used to work beaded lines onto the surface of the knitting and can work well when combined with other embroidery techniques.

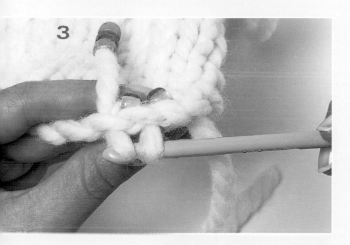

1 Thread the beads onto the yarn and pull a 4–6 in. (10–15 cm) tail of yarn through to the wrong side of fabric, between the first and second stitches, so that the working yarn with beads is on the right side.

2 Push the first bead along the yarn up to the knitting and push the hook up from the wrong side between the second and third stitches pulling a loop of yarn through to the wrong side, holding the bead in place.

3 Push the next bead along the yarn to the knitting and pull another loop of yarn through to the wrong side, holding the second bead in place. There are now two loops on the hook.

4 Pull the new loop through the first loop, leaving one loop on the hook.

5 Repeat steps 3 and 4 along the edge to be beaded. Make sure that you keep the chain that is formed on the wrong side quite loose, as if it is worked too tightly the knitting will be pulled out of shape.

PROJECT 14: Sequinned Shawl

This glittering shawl will put your scarf to the back of the closet! Giant-sized sequins are easily knitted into the zigzag chevron design, adding sparkle to the vivid mohair. You may wish to further exaggerate the chevron and experiment striping with different colored mohair. Have a look back at the suggestions for Project 9: Lacy Cowl Neck to get some ideas for how this may look.

Materials
660 yds (600 m) luxury chunky mohair yarn
300 giant sequins divided into 60 each of colors A, B, C, D, and E.
1 pair size 11 (7 mm) knitting needles
Tapestry needle

Gauge
Over stockinette stitch on size 11 (7 mm) needles:
  12 stitches and 15 rows to 4 in. (10 cm)

Finished measurements
Width 24 in. (60 cm)
Length at side edge 63 in. (160) cm

Abbreviations
k–knit; **p**–purl; **ws**–wrong side; **rs**–right side
k2tog–knit two stitches together; **yf**–bring yarn forward to make a yarn over; **rpt**–repeat;
st(s)–stitch(es); **sl1**–slip one stitch; **yb**–take yarn to back of work

Before knitting
Divide sequins into groups of 15 for each stripe. You may decide to mix colors randomly, but keeping each group of 15 sequins as a single color will give a clearer chevron stripe effect

Thread sequins onto the first ball of yarn. (See page 112.)
You will have to estimate how many rows can be knitted with the first ball of yarn. But if you thread all the sequins for the first 5 stripes onto a 110 yd (100 m) ball of yarn, you should not run out of sequins. If you do, simply break the yarn at the end of a row and re-thread more sequins. If the yarn runs out, re-thread the sequins in the correct order onto the next ball of yarn. Remember that the sequins need to be threaded in the reverse order to the way that you knit them. Therefore the last 15 sequins that you thread onto the ball will be color A, the first stripe of sequins to be knitted, and so on.

To make the shawl
Cast on 83 stitches on size 11 (7 mm) needles.
Work 4 rows garter stitch (plain knitting).
With ws facing, work sequin chevron pattern as follows:

Five closely spaced sequin stripes:
Sequin chevron pattern
Row 1 K4, p to last 4 sts, k4.
Row 2 K4, (k2tog, k10, yf, k1, yf, k10, k2tog), rpt to last 4 sts, k4.
Row 3 K4, p to last 4 sts, k4.
Row 4 K4, (k2, yf with sequin color A, sl1, yb, k2), rpt to last 4 sts, k4.
Row 5 K4, p to last 4 sts, k4.
Row 6 K4, (k2tog, k10, yf, k1, yf, k10, k2tog), rpt to last 4 sts, k4.
Rows 7–12 Work chevron pattern from row 1–6, using color B sequins on row 10.
Rows 13–18 Work chevron pattern from row 1–6, using color C sequins on row 16.
Rows 19–24 Work chevron pattern from row 1–6, using color D sequins on row 22.
Rows 25–30 Work chevron pattern from row 1–6, using color E sequins on row 28.

Five widely spaced sequin stripes:
Non-sequin chevron pattern
Row 31 K4, p to last 4 sts, k4.
Row 32 K4, (k2tog, k10, yf, k1, yf, k10, k2tog), rpt to last 4 sts, k4.
Row 33 K4, p to last 4 sts, k4.
Row 34 K all stitches.
Row 35 K4, p to last 4 sts, k4.

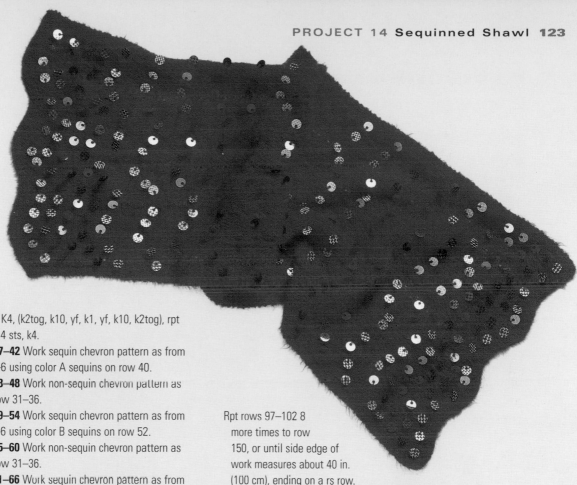

Row 36 K4, (k2tog, k10, yf, k1, yf, k10, k2tog), rpt to last 4 sts, k4.

Rows 37–42 Work sequin chevron pattern as from row 1–6 using color A sequins on row 40.

Rows 43–48 Work non-sequin chevron pattern as from row 31–36.

Rows 49–54 Work sequin chevron pattern as from row 1–6 using color B sequins on row 52.

Rows 55–60 Work non-sequin chevron pattern as from row 31–36.

Rows 61–66 Work sequin chevron pattern as from row 1–6, using color C sequins on row 64.

Rows 67–72 Work non-sequin chevron pattern as from row 31–36.

Rows 73–78 Work sequin chevron pattern as from row 1–6 using color D sequins on row 76.

Rows 79–84 Work non-sequin chevron pattern as from row 31–36.

Rows 85–90 Work sequin chevron pattern as from row 1–6 using color E sequins on row 88.

Rows 91–96 Work non-sequin chevron pattern, as from row 31–36.

Central chevron section without sequins

Non-sequin chevron pattern

Row 97 K4, p to last 4 sts, k4.

Row 98 K4, (k2tog, k10, yf, k1, yf, k10, k2tog), rpt to last 4 sts, k4.

Row 99 K4, p to last 4 sts, k4.

Row 100 K all stitches.

Row 101 K4, p to last 4 sts, k4.

Row 102 K4, (k2tog, k10, yf, k1, yf, k10, k2tog), rpt to last 4 sts, k4.

Rpt rows 97–102 8 more times to row 150, or until side edge of work measures about 40 in. (100 cm), ending on a rs row.

Five widely spaced sequin stripes

Row 151–210 Rpt rows 37–96, striping sequins in same order, colors A–E.

Five closely spaced sequin stripes

Row 211–240 Rpt rows 1–30, striping sequins in same order, colors A–E.

Row 241 K4, p to last 4, k4.

Garter stitch edge

Work 4 rows garter stitch.
Bind off knitwise.

Finishing

Work in all loose ends.

Block, pulling chevron edge to shape, using damp spray method, and if desired brush gently with mohair brush on right side, being careful not to catch sequins.

CHUNKY KNITS

Decorative Details

The vibrant mohair is enlivened by the addition of shiny and colorful sequins. To add an even bigger splash of color, try adding the loopy sequinned fringe at either end or all around the shawl, using a crochet hook. The sequins on the shawl are knitted in using the basic slipstitch technique explained in Decadent Touch Techniques, but more sequins can be added as a trim after the shawl has been knitted. The shawl pattern can also be adapted using knotted lengths of colorful ribbon for a decorative zigzag stripe detail as an alternative to the sequins.

Sequin fringe

Prepare the yarn by threading on sufficient sequins. Allow about 1 sequin and 4 in. (10 cm) of yarn per ½ in. (1 cm) of edge to be trimmed. Use a crochet hook of a similar size to the knitting needles used.

1 Hold the shawl edge with the right side facing you, and the end of the sequinned yarn behind, in one hand. Hold the crochet hook in the other hand. Push the hook through the knitting, in the middle of the edge stitch, and pull a loop of yarn through to the right side.

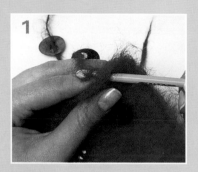

2 Make a big loop of working yarn with a sequin on it, around your raised index finger. Push the hook through the middle of the next stitch at the edge of the knitting and catch the yarn at the front of the loop.

3 Pull the yarn from the front of the loop, through the knitting, so there are two stitches on the hook.

4 Push the hook through the middle of the next stitch of the knitting, and catch the yarn, this time at the back of the loop that is round your index finger.

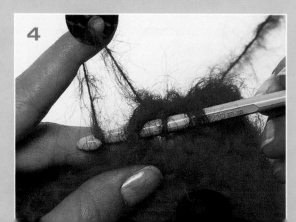

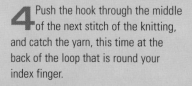

5 Pull the yarn through the knitting and through both stitches on the hook, leaving one stitch on the hook. Remove your finger from the loop, ready to make the next loop.

6 Repeat the process from step 2, working along the edge to be fringed, one loop at a time. Slide a new sequin along the yarn and into position as each loop is wrapped around your finger. At the end of the trim, break the yarn and pull the end through the last stitch to secure.

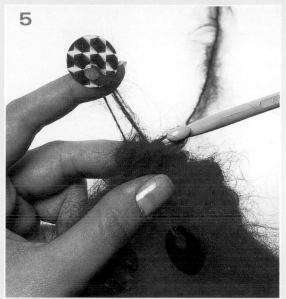

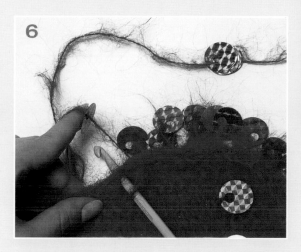

Knotted ribbon stripe detail

Ribbon is a traditional and useful trim for knitwear, often used threaded through eyelets and as drawstrings and bows. A more contemporary use for ribbon is to knit it in, using it as a luxurious and decorative yarn. Lengths of colorful ribbon can be knotted and knitted to make a decorative garter stitch edge, and as a narrow contrast stripe pattern picking out the chevron design. Shiny satin ribbon makes an exciting complement to mohair, but can also be used in combination with other yarns.

Choose a ribbon width that will work with your needle size.

A width of ⅛ in. (3 mm) is suitable for use with the mohair shawl. Knot together assorted lengths—between about 20 cm (8 in.) and 1 m (39 in.)—of colorful ribbons to create your own yarn. The knots form part of the fabric, so tie very firmly and trim the ends evenly. If the ribbon is very slippery, dampen the knot before tightening—this will make it more secure. Roll the knotted ribbon yarn into a small ball or around a bobbin, so that it is easy to work with. The garter stitch cast-on and bound-off edges can be worked in ribbon, for a decorative, textured trim. The pattern can be worked without slipping stitches and adding sequins – instead try knitting a two-row stripe of garter stitch with the ribbon.

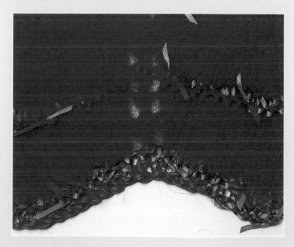

Reading Patterns

When you first look at a knitting pattern it can seem confusing because of the abbreviations used. However, patterns are actually written in a very logical order so that they are simple to follow, and the same terms and abbreviations are used in different patterns. Read a pattern through before you start knitting to make sure that you understand all the instructions and have the necessary materials and equipment.

Abbreviations and terminology

Many instructions are abbreviated and are usually explained at the beginning of the pattern. Most abbreviations are standard and you will soon find that you have become familiar with them. However, always check carefully because there can be some variation from pattern to pattern and similar abbreviations could be confused.

Some of the more commonly used abbreviations are listed here.

alt–alternate

beg–beginning

BO–bind off

C4F or **C4L**–cable stitches at front

C4B or **C4R**–cable stitches at back

CC–contrast color

CO–cast on

col–color

cm–centimeters

cont–continue

dec–decrease/decreasing

dpn–double-pointed needles

foll–following

G, **gr**, or **gm**–grams

G st–garter stitch

in.–inches

inc–increase/increasing

k–knit

kfb–knit into front and back of stitch (increasing)

k2tog–knit 2 together

LH–left hand

lp–loop

meas–measures

m–meters

MC–main color

m1–make 1

oz–ounce(s)

p–purl

pfb–purl into front and back of same stitch

pat(t)–pattern

psso–pass slipstitch(es) over

p2tog–purl 2 together

rem–remaining

rpt (or** rep)**–repeat

rev st.st–reverse stockinette stitch

RH–right hand

rib–ribbing

rs–right side

sl–slip

sl1, k1, psso–slip 1, knit 1, pass slipstitch over

sl st–slipstitch

st–stitch(es)

st.st–stockinette stitch

tbl–through back loop

tog–together

ws –wrong side

wyib–with yarn in back

wyif–with yarn in front

yd(s)–yard(s)

yf–yarn to the front between needles

yo or **yon**–yarn over needle (to make extra stitch)

" –inches

*** or ( )**–asterisks or parentheses are used to show a set of instructions that need to be repeated a stated amount of times.

Charts

Instructions may be given as text or may refer to a chart, with a key explaining symbols used. Charts are often provided for multicolored, Fair Isle, and intarsia knitting, or for textured knits such as lace or cable. Each square represents a stitch and the chart should be read from the bottom right-hand corner. All odd numbered rows (usually right side) should be read from right to left, while even numbered rows are read from left to right.

Measurements and sizing

Actual measurements of finished garments are given.

Chest/bust measurement This is usually the width of the front plus the width of the back.

Garment length This measurement is given from the highest shoulder point or from the center back neck point to the bottom edge of the garment.

Sleeve length This measurement is usually taken from the cuff edge to the point where underarm shaping begins. The measurement is taken vertically, not along the shaped seam edge.

Where a choice of sizes is included in a pattern, the instructions for these are usually given throughout the pattern in parentheses, in order of size, with the smallest size first. Where only one figure is given, it applies across all sizes.

Materials

Pattern instructions will list the quantity and type of yarn needed, the recommended needle size, and any other requirements, such as buttons and zippers.

Gauge

It is important to follow the given gauge (see page 28).

Knitting the garment pieces

Most garment instructions list the pieces in the order to be knitted: back, front, sleeves, and then neckbands and trims, which may be listed as part of "Finishing" or "Assembling."

Finishing

Instructions will be given for blocking and assembling your garment. Remember to refer to the ball band of your yarn at this stage.

Adapting patterns

Because each knitted garment is created individually, it can be possible to adjust a pattern to suit your own requirements. It is important that the correct gauge is achieved. If your knitting does not exactly match the correct gauge, the garment will not assemble to the correct size and the shape may be distorted. Some designs can be too complicated to adapt, but the length of an area of knitting that does not have shaping can be easily adjusted. It is more complicated to adjust the width, so it is recommended to work with a pattern and gauge that knits to the desired width (correct number of stitches over desired measurement). To adjust the length, use the gauge of the test swatch to recalculate the number of rows needed. Some patterns give a finished length to be knitted rather than stating a number of rows required as it can be important to achieve the correct length. When adjusting patterns with stitch structure or Fair Isle designs, try to adapt the length by adding or subtracting a whole pattern repeat.

Yarns used in this Book

The patterns in this book list generic yarn types. Below is a description of the specific yarn brands that were used for the patterns. If you need to buy a substitute yarn, use this information as a guide, bearing in mind that the key measurement is the yardage (metrage) per weight of ball or hank.

Chunky wool yarn (Project 6)
Cygnet Wool Rich Chunky *75% wool; 25% polyamide*
Approx. 135 yds (162m) per 50g ball

Chunky wool yarn (Project 7)
Rowanspun Chunky *100% wool*
Approx. 142 yds (130m) per 100g hank

Chunky wool yarn (Project 8)
Rowan Cork *90% wool; 10% nylon*
Approx. 120 yds (110 m) per 50g ball

Extra chunky machine-washable wool mix yarn (Projects 3, 11)
Sirdar Nova *50% wool; 50% acrylic*
Approx. 124yds (113 m) per 100g ball

Extra chunky wool fleece yarn (Project 7)
Jaeger Natural Fleece *100% wool*
Approx 93 yds (85 m) per 100g

Extra chunky wool mix yarn (Project 10)
Rowan Polar *60% wool; 30% alpaca; 10% acrylic*
Approx. 110 yds (100m) per 100g ball

Fisherman (Aran) yarn (Project 6)
Debbie Bliss Merino Aran *100% Merino wool*
Approx. 85 yds (78 m) per 50g ball

Luxury chunky mohair yarn (Project 10)
Hayfield Luxury Mohair *80% mohair yarn; 10% nylon; 10% acrylic*
Approx. 111 yds (101 m) per 50g ball

Luxury chunky mohair yarn (Project 14)
Papillon Mohair *82% mohair; 9% wool; 9% nylon*
Approx. 108 yds (98 m) per 50g ball

Super chunky slubby wool yarn (Project 1)
Rowan Biggy Print *100% merino wool*
Approx. 33 yds (30 m) per 100g ball

Super chunky slubby wool yarn (hand dyed) (Project 5)
Colinette Point 5 *100% wool*
Approx. 55 yds (50 m) per 100g hank

Super chunky wool yarn (Projects 1, 4, 12, 13)
Rowan Big Wool *100% merino wool*
Approx. 87 yds (80 m) per 100g ball

Super chunky wool mix yarn (Project 2)
Patons Funky Chunky *60% wool; 40% acrylic*
Approx. 42 yds (38 m) per 50g ball

CHUNKY KNITS

Index & credits

abbreviations 127
Afghan Coat 72–75

backstitch seam 31
beaded edge, crochet 121
beaded lace holes 120
Beaded Sweater 116–119
beads, to knit in 112–113
belt loops 77
binding off 22
Blackberry Bomber 64–69
blackberry popcorn stitch 58–59
blocking 29
Bomber, Blackberry 64–69
button stand 71
buttonhole 40
    band 71
buttons, to attach 57

cable techniques 58, 62–63
    double 92
    single rib 93
Cable V-neck 88–91
Cardigan, Chunky 52–55
    Snowflake 99–102
casting on 16–17
chart: color knitting 103
    lace 87
    to read 127
Chunky Cardigan 52–55
Coat, Afghan 72–75
cord, twisted 76
cotton yarn 10
crochet: beaded edge 121
    chain stitch embroidery 115
    hook 13
    ties 41

decreasing: left-sloping 27
    right-sloping 26
design, to adapt 86

embroidery techniques 111, 114–115
eyelet hole 40

faggot lace 59
Fair Isle 94–95
fastenings: buttons and buttonholes 40, 57,
    71
    ties 41, 76, 77, 80
    zipper 70
flowers, knitted 81

garter stitch 18
    neckband 51
gauge 10, 11, 28, 126

Hippie Shoulder Bag 38–39

increasing: bar 23–24
    lifted strand 25
    multiple stitch 25
intarsia knitting 13, 96–97, 110

Kids' Poncho 78–79
knit stitch 18
knitting pattern : to adapt 126
    to read 126–127

lace holes 59
    beaded 120
    chart 87
    on rib 87
Lacy Cowl Neck Sweater 82–85
laddering 50
Ladies' Turtleneck Raglan 48–49

Man's Intarsia Sweater 106–109
Man's Raglan Rollover 42–45
mattress stitch seam 30–31, 47

needles: cable 12, 58
    to hold 15
    length 12, 14
    sizes 10, 11, 28
    types 12

picking up stitches 46–47
pockets: to inset 56
    to oversew 37
pompoms 105
    textured 93
Poncho, Kids' 78–79
poodle loop stitch 60–61
purl stitch 19

Raglan, Ladies' Turtleneck 48–49
Raglan, Man's Rollover 42–45
rib: double 20
    single 20
    two-color 104

Scarf, Woolly Winter 34–35
seams 30–31
    cuff 47
seed stitch 21
selvage, to trim 57
sequin(s): fringe 124
    to knit in 112–113
Sequinned Shawl 122–125
shaping see decreasing; increasing
Shawl, Sequinned 122–125
Shoulder Bag, Hippie 38–39

Ski Hat, Simple 98–99
slip knot 14
Snowflake Style 98–102
stockinette stitch 20
    flowers 81
    reverse 20
stranding 94
sweaters: Beaded Sweater 116–119
    Cable V-neck 88–91
    Lacy Cowl Neck Sweater 82–85
    Ladies' Turtleneck Raglan 48–49
    Man's Intarsia Sweater 106–109
    Man's Raglan Rollover 42–45
swiss darning 111

threading detail 92
ties: corded 76, 77
    crochet 41
    leafy 80

V-neck, Cable 88–91

weaving in: in Fair Isle 95
    in intarsia 110
    yarn ends 29, 36
Woolly Winter Scarf 34–35

yarn: to carry at back of work 94, 95
    to carry up side of work 57
    fiber 10
    to hold 15
    to join 21
    to organize for intarsia 110
    to substitute 28
    weights 10–11
yarn ends, to weave in 29, 36
    in intarsia 110
yarnover technique 40, 59

Credits

Quarto would like to thank Karolina Bacinska,
Matt Dolphin, Charlotte Knight, Laura
Montesanti, and Elena Timofeeva for modeling
the projects in this book, and Sheilla Sandalha
for hand-modeling the techniques. All
photographs and illustrations are the
copyright of Quarto.

Author's Acknowledgments

A big thanks to all the enthusiastic knitters
who worked on the projects in this book—
Helen Clewer, Tiphaine de Lussy, Carol
Barnard, Carolyne Ekong, Amanda
Griffiths, and Sandra Brown.